Graffiti in Eden

Finding Peace through Sex, Love and Infidelity

Angela J Engel

Her co-author wishes to remain anonymous

Printed in the United States

ISBN 978-1-7339292-0-2
Library of Congress Control Number: 2019903927

E-book ISBN 978-1-7339292-1-9

Author Photograph by Angela Terrell
Cover Photograph by Steven Plant
Cover design by Goran Tovilovic

Visit me on the web!
www.AngelaEngel.com
www.GraffitiInEden.com

For J.T.

Whether we are pirouetting in the sunlight or
wrestling in the shadows—
There is only grace.

Author's Note

Here among these pages is a different story than the one we grew up hearing. It did not happen in a land far, far away. It happened right next door. Although two people did meet and they did fall in love, in this story they fell in love while married to someone else.

The villains and monsters they battled were within themselves and the victories...still undecided. Still there are pirate captains and gypsy queens. Treasures are won...and lost. Amid the cul-de-sacs and mini-vans you may find a castle, a moat, and a sorceress, too.

The man drinking coffee across from you may in fact be a cheating pirate captain. A gypsy charlatan queen may be sitting next to you in the church pew, minus her panties. While we still hold to the fairy tale ideals of marriage, love is a bit more complicated. Often it is easier to live in reality while dabbling in fantasy. On rare occasions, such as this, the two collide.

CHAPTER ONE

He came to me early in spring along with the song birds returning from their winter havens. I simply opened my e-mail one morning and there was his name staring back at me, Thomas Wright. I recall the sensation, briefly awakened from my dullness as if the universe wanted to alert me something important was about to occur.

More than seven years have passed since the first email and the substance of being together has cast a shadow of vagueness on how we first got here. Although the specifics escape me, I remember the pretense, he and his wife were having difficulty and he was hoping I could help.

I knew his wife. We had become friends more than a decade earlier. We were not best friends but certainly more than acquaintances. Our lives had followed a similar path: teaching, marriage, and children. Our friendship had weathered the years and that was enough. Despite Thomas's assertions, he claimed to be looking for advice, I knew exactly where he was aiming. It was not the first time someone's husband had approached me. The justifications were different, their hopes often the same. I quickly responded to Mr. Thomas Wright, "I am not interested in any type of encounter."

My initial resistance did not have anything to do with attraction. If he had not been married, I would have otherwise been interested. He is certainly my type—a Harley riding Ph.D. with a social conscience. I know the indicator of my approval system, a small flutter dancing inside.

At 6'1" with broad shoulders, bright blue eyes, and a perfectly shaped bald head, Thomas has a commanding presence. Our first introduction the decade earlier was not necessarily memorable. Several years of my life were spent sleepwalking. In those earlier years I noticed very little, this chapter may be called "youth."

At later events I remember glancing to see if he was watching me or stealing a peek to capture small details—the shape of his jaw line, straightness of his teeth, or the possibility of chest hair. Although it was not the kind of crush keeping me up nights, during the rare occasions we saw each other throughout the years, I became increasingly more alert to his presence. At holiday gatherings or a birthday party, I began to notice how he possessed a rare combination of strength and sensitivity. I would watch how he would stay apart from the group and yet observe in a way that made him a full participant. His quiet confidence offered the answer to a secret you didn't know you were missing.

The subconscious is powerful and so I must accept blame. I recall how, in anticipation of seeing him at an upcoming Christmas party, I gave special attention to selecting my holiday dress. I chose a chestnut brown satin gown to match the color of my eyes. The fabric wrapped tightly around my bodice, leaving my shoulders exposed with my quiet hope his eyes would seek the bareness of my skin.

DREAMS AND DUST

In the beginning, I remember thinking how I had achieved everything I could want—more than any man could expect, really. By all accounts I should have been the happiest son-of-a-bitch alive. I started with nothing, absolutely nothing, and created a reality out of dust and dreams. I earned my doctorate, ran a successful practice, married a princess bride, built a home, and witnessed the birth of the two most beautiful angels to grace the earth.

Still, deeper down, I never really sought the kind of success driven by "the Great American Dream," of more money, bigger cars, or important titles. I never gave a damn about any of those. To me, all of the hours of graduate school and building a business and creating a home weren't about proving myself. Not to anybody. To me, success just meant I could finally live on my own time—no clocks to punch and no reporting to any "superior." I stood on the front lawn wearing hand painted armor and shook my cardboard sword at all the absent fathers as they drove to some ridiculous downtown cubicle. This was my success.

Sarah, my wife, did not share my definition of accomplished. She cared mostly for appearances, everything on the surface. She valued the right house in the right neighborhood with the right friends from the right church attending the right gatherings.

From the moment I first saw her, I truly believed love would carry us forever. Until gradually, minute by minute, hour by hour, as the years passed it became abundantly clear the attraction was not mutual. Nothing I said, or did, or romanced would ever result in the kind of intimacy I craved. Not because she didn't want to. I know, in her way and in her mind she loved me to the best of her ability. I simply recognized she wasn't capable of reaching the deep intimacy I sought.

About a decade into my marriage I realized we had only been playing house. Josephine may not remember how we got here, but I do. I was balancing on the precipice of what felt like life and death. I was desperate to touch something hot and volatile. I went looking for danger because I wanted to feel alive.

The drive to the banquet hall this evening involved the usual quiet distance, another silent approach to another meaningless engagement while the seconds ticked away as infinite as ever, despite the short distance. Ordinarily I would give my wife some excuse to be absent from this type of social obligation—holiday celebrations full of forced smiles, gaudy presentments, and the characters overdressed, overindulged. Except on this night, I knew she would be there. I perched myself on a bar stool in full view of the entrance. A half hour passed and I was looking at the ice cubes in my empty drink when I felt her enter the dining hall in a short brown satin dress.

Josephine fills a room, radiant and beautiful, with a razor wit beneath her raw intelligence. She masters her audience instantly. Conversation takes a breath when she arrives and her charisma is impossible to resist. Men invariably tilt their attention toward her, thinking, "God damn! What I wouldn't give…" Women subject themselves in their own, more subtle ways, from fear, or envy, or respect. No one walks away from Josephine feeling something commonplace has just passed.

They buzz in diminishing circles around her and she accepts them. She intoxicates them—Josephine with her exotic penetrating eyes and rapturous smile. Her rhythm is in the moment. People hesitate, glancing toward their spouses. They try to account for her and fall short. She is a visionary more than capable of raising the conversation to a level where you realize you haven't quite done your homework, regardless of the topic.

I succumb to the irresistible urge to melt into a corner and watch.

CHAPTER TWO

During the holiday party, I catch him watching me. Thomas is fearless. In the past he at least attempted to conceal his attraction, not tonight. At previous events we often engaged in idle conversation. Most impressionable were the words unspoken. Despite his brazen stares, on this night he merely flashes a smile of recognition while never approaching.

So it came as rather a surprise when late in March on a sunny and still-cold morning his name appeared in my inbox. He had hit a wall in his marriage, he wrote, and he was seeking my perspective, my insight. He knew my husband and I had created a different kind of marital union and removed the barriers of monogamy while creating an honest and intimate partnership. He also trusted my woman's perspective, and he knew I had a personal insight into his wife.

It was written to appear as an honest and sincere request *for answers. I was familiar with people asking questions; I give direction for a living. Still, my initial reply established the boundaries. I would offer some suggestions through email. I refused to meet in person, clearly establishing the limits and ensuring there would be no potential for sex.*

At first I naively confessed the exchange to my husband, Vince, thinking nothing would come of a brief e-mail chat. I am not the virtuous type, quite the opposite, actually. I did, however, have one rule: I do not get involved with other women's men. I had prided my-

self on holding this line. I considered myself loyal to the sisterhood, and the role of "the other woman" was simply something I could not accept.

Because the Internet offers the illusion of safety, I played along. It started harmlessly. He asked interesting questions. He challenged me with engaging problems, ones worth solving. "What does one do in a marriage when you love your spouse and realize what you want most she cannot give?" "How can two people live together and yet feel utterly alone?" "Where do you go when your hopes and dreams have changed, but your responsibilities have stayed the same?" "Who am I?" "Why are we here?" "What is it all for?"

I am a lover of words which is how Thomas courted me. He used to write me long e-mails in the middle of the night, and I would wake to the anticipation of his poetry across my screen. Those ended when my husband began reading my e-mails. What he read or did not read, I will never know.

I love men. It is not that I do not see them for who they are, I do. I just forgive them. I once had dinner with some girlfriends and the single women were asking the married women the question, "What does a man really want?" Some of the women in the group went on proselytizing about blow jobs, affirming egos, companionship, and so forth. Others had more enlightened responses, "Men want connection, partnership, and the opportunity to know themselves deeply and honestly." I waited and listened. Eventually the single women began looking more confused and distraught. I spoke up. "Women make relationships far too complicated," I said. "Men want to eat, sleep, and have sex, and they want the woman who makes all of those tasks the easiest and most fun." Of course the human psyche is far more complex than this, and there is a vast range relating to man's evolution. However, if you remember that we are first hostage to our own biology, this answer makes perfect sense. Men are even more primitive than women.

Marriage was never my goal, although my marital union was arranged by the time I was eighteen. Not by our families or a church, rather by the stars and universe who chooses our partners long before we recognize them ourselves. I will save this story for another time. What I am simply meaning to say is, who I am and my relationships will not fit into your current schema of wife, marriage, or motherhood. I seem to violate all notions of "tradition" and go about life defining my own roles and rules in the world.

I first made love before my sixteenth birthday. Of course my sexual introduction was not a wise love. It was the teenage, naïve, innocent kind of love only children can believe. The attraction was not instantaneous. It was his personality that won me over. He was caring and protective, eventually I wanted to lie naked with our bodies pressed together. For months he caressed me, held me, and kissed my forehead and all my other parts. Eventually I invited him to enter the secret part of me. Our bodies coming together where our hearts had already met brought me both joy and pleasure. I have had bad sexual experiences with bad characters in my earlier years. You can learn as much from the ugliness as you can from the beauty. I am a quick learner, and because my parents approached the subject of sexuality with openness and acceptance and because of the tenderness in my first experiences, sex has always been an affirming element of my life.

In truth, I did not have very many partners early in my development. Vince proposed before my twentieth birthday and we were married four months after I earned my first college degree. My sexual awakening came later after my children were born. I still remember the year I entered my womanhood. I was past thirty and discovering my body beyond that of host. My hips were done birthing, my breasts were done nursing, and there came a stirring buried deep behind and below my navel. Vince had seen me too long as wife and mother and could not see me for the sexual vessel I longed to be.

I found the man who would introduce me to my new sensuality lifting weights at the athletic club in the primal atmosphere of perspiration and heavy breathing. He was recently divorced. We spent months watching each other in the steamy mirrors before the first word was spoken. His name was Jason. He was the perfect combination of gentleman and fighter. He had grown up in New Jersey, and despite the rough-and-tumble bloody brawls of growing up, he had carved out a clean living wearing suits and ties. Even the crookedness from a broken nose had been surgically straightened to a perfect edge.

The only remaining sign of Jason's dark side was a Celtic braid tattoo wrapped around his gorgeous bicep. Even today I moisten at the thought of those black outlines crisply carved into the bulging taut muscle holding my arms in place above my head. When our bodies finally connected, the power surging between us was transformative. I remember him shaking when we kissed, and I remember vividly my own shaking when I came beneath him. The affair was short-lived. He welcomed me into womanhood, and I alleviated his grief and restored his optimism toward a promising future.

Now I seem to attract a new lover every year. Once you heed the serpent's temptation, it is difficult to return to the hobbies of knitting and ceramics.

A LIFE AND A WIFE

It began like most marriages, I suppose. I fell in love. Not like before—I mean, I fell in love with Sarah immediately. It was the kind of attraction they try to capture in the movies. I could see the future even before our first kiss. She was the ideal I had pictured.

I realize now how I need challenge. Difficulty inspires me, it's probably the source of my own downfall. I can be relentless when properly challenged, and oh, God, how she challenged me. Twenty years ago, she stood before me unattainable and pristine. I really thought I'd eventually win her in the end. I truly did. If only I could just release her passion—the barrier beneath her need to color inside the lines. How incredible it would be to witness her vulnerability beyond the rote repression and self-imposed good girl image. I longed for her single, pure moment of abandonment and, finally, any hint of surrender.

That's not what happened. The months simply ticked away, and all my efforts to overcome her barriers were defeated. And slowly, I began to lose heart. Until one day her passion finally unleashed with her longing to be a mother. The fortress fell and for the briefest of moments I actually believed we'd broken through. Never had she been more desirous. Never had she shown me such interest and availability than when she wanted and then carried our child.

I rediscovered joy during those early blissful years when

I submitted to fatherhood and the family entrusted to me. When the second was conceived, I already knew it was over. I had played my role. Her passion ceased the moment her goal was achieved. She had secured her future, and once again my every advance would meet the same impenetrable wall.

I remember reading a magazine several months after the birth of our first son. I hate magazine articles on principle, because they say nothing and simply try to tweak emotions like shock and fear. Still, this one caught my attention, and the fact I recall it all these years later gives some testament to the time. It's no surprise it was a piece on sex after childbirth. The lingering statement was apparently supposed to be an encouragement to new fathers. "Don't worry, it could take up to four weeks before your partner feels intimate after giving birth. There are many changes happening…" Four weeks? A month? I was driven to hysterics and threw the magazine across the room. Five months had passed without a single sexually intimate gesture. I turned my attention to my sons and gave up the pursuit.

Sarah eventually noticed. I remember our conversation and how she cried and begged me "not to leave the responsibility in her hands," and all I could think was, "Why not? You've left it in my hands for our entire marriage."

It's possible I should have left my marriage then, honestly the idea didn't even cross my mind. In spite of every broken dream, there is an unshakable truth about marriage and family. With the promise to spend every day beside each other, we ought to be damn well prepared to learn and live with all of the best and worst a spouse has to offer. And it would be in anyone's best interest to know the worst is going to hurt. It's going to sear and expose our hidden wounds and shadowy fears.

That's true of anyone, especially those inclined with the courage to walk a lifelong path with a partner. The real gift in relationships is we have the opportunity to master forgiveness, to understand how our own faults and flaws amount to the same or even more hurtful wounds than those we choose to endure. The story of love we're never told is the price of growth—the kind of life alteration which leaves you still standing…naked and ready to learn.

I still couldn't have seen or imagined how it would all turn out.

Since seeing Josephine at the Christmas party, even before then, I had been planning to reach out to her. I was ready to toss aside every preconceived notion of acceptable platitudes and connect to something real and honest.

So I wrote without any real idea of the forces which drove me to her. Looking back through a cloudy lens, what I sought most was a simple connection beyond the unrelenting silent desperation of marriage. I was starving for some confirmation of meaning and the need to experience life on its own terms.

I wrote to her online, a safe, discrete sort of note. A reach into the cosmos for something beyond all I then held sacred. Oh, I had questions for Josephine, yet the answers weren't where I was looking.

I was quite aware of our connection—untested, but I knew. I look back realizing the attraction had always been there. Through brief snapshots in time we had shared intimate niceties at family picnics, dinner parties, and holiday venues. I already knew her.

CHAPTER THREE

My rules did not matter to Thomas; resistance is exactly the type of prompting that most excites him. I was a fly in his web all the while thinking I was the spider. Silly girl! He asked me to meet him for coffee or a drink. I refused. In my mind, the distance kept me separate. I have spent decades constructing protective shields. I believed my heart to be safe. I tricked myself into thinking as long as we did not touch bodies, I was not in fact deceiving a friend, betraying a husband, or eventually falling in love.

People often compliment my physical appearance. Once a woman has grown comfortable in herself, physical beauty is rather irrelevant. While at first they may be seduced by the softness of my curves, it is something entirely different attracting these men. I live life fearlessly and with an open invitation followed with gratitude, regardless of the experience. They see the conscious life coursing through my veins, and they want to drink from the river of eternal hope and abandon. Thomas, having heard the Greek myth of the siren song, nevertheless set his bow toward me. After eleven months of phone calls and e-mails, temptation overtakes my moral high ground and I surrender. Finally, I give in to the need to watch Thomas's mouth as he speaks the words which have entranced me. When I explain Vince will be in New York the coming week, he asks me if I would like to meet him for a drink. This time to both our surprise, I reply, "Yes."

On a Wednesday evening after finishing with his last client,

Thomas picks me up. In the walk from my front door to his car, I feel like a little school girl trying to conceal the twitch in my smile. He is wearing a white dress shirt perfectly pressed.

I like a well-dressed man. I can smell Thomas the moment I climb into his SUV. He does not smell of cologne or aftershave; he smells of laundry detergent and Dial soap. It is subtle and fresh and offers the assurance—if you bury your face in his chest, and it is the hairy type, you will not be overpowered with artificial perfumes, rather the scent of man.

The part that will forever remain in my memory of our first encounter is the moment when we first looked into each other's eyes and how he slid his fingers through the back of my hair and drew me in to kiss him. It was so fluid, like he had kissed me this way every day for the whole of our lives.

I had not planned for us to kiss. I wanted to be near him, and somewhere inside I knew the danger of this encounter, and the part of me I like best hoped for a simple friendship. I had waited eleven months and I idealistically hoped a platonic relationship was possible. Thomas set the tone immediately. From the moment he kissed me, the polite amicability of friendship was gone forever. We were lovers from the instant our lips touched, and quite possibly before.

So with me safely belted beside him, we drove to a trendy restaurant called Vernon's. Eighty-five percent of the clientele are business men. One hundred percent of the wait staff are women. You know the kind of place, sex really does sell. The men leaned back in dark leather benches or cherry-stained stools watching basketball, golf, and race car driving on eighteen carefully positioned plasma flat screens. They watched something else too…out of the corner of their eyes they followed the beautiful young waitresses in their short skirts and Victoria's Secret push-up bras.

We chose a small round table with two wingback library chairs. The nearby gas fireplace matched the character of the bar patrons, a bright, elegant imitation. Vernon's is always crowded and a good place to study facades.

Thomas did not see the lonely swirls of Makers Mark Whiskey or the blonde hair flip. He watched only me. I sized him up as well, clean shaven, nice pants; I mentioned the shirt already. His brown suede loafers were the only thing alarming me, and fortunately they lingered out of view under the table.

I listened carefully as he ordered. I can read a man in the way he orders:

Does he make eye contact?

Is he decisive?

Are the words "please" and "thank you" applied gener ously or appropriately?

Does he speak for his date?

Does he smile?

Back then I was the twenty-question girl. I would even send the waitress back with special instructions for the chef: "Dressing on the side, olive oil instead of butter please, may I have this vegetable, and does this sauce...?" It is possible to irritate even ourselves.

Now, years after our first date at Vernon's, Thomas gives the waitress my order. He asks me what I want first. If I do not know, then when the waitress comes I ask my questions and he follows up with a recommendation she come back in a couple of minutes. I talk through the dining dilemmas and menu selections, and when she returns, he recites my order. I love it! On special occasions when he has trouble deciding what to eat, he asks me to choose, and I do the ordering for both of us. I love that, too.

Of course, I've gotten ahead of myself again. On our first date, Thomas did not order for me. When the waitress arrived, she asked, "Would you like to start with some drinks?"

Thomas, smiling, directed his gaze toward me.

(The chivalrous type.)

"I'd like the Pinot Noir, please," I answer.

Thomas orders his favorite micro-brew.

(Dependable.)

"I'm sorry, sir, we don't carry that. But we have a sun shine wheat that's pretty similar."

Without disguising his irritation, he says, "Hmm, okay, I'll try it."

(Honest, expressive, risk-taker.)

When she comes back with our drink order, he politely thanks her, smiling again.
(Forgives easily.)

Now that the ordering assessment is over, I settle into the back of my chair and take stock of his physical presence. His body language is relaxed, his facial expressions are attentive. He freely initiates conversation and listens equally. At 45, he is nearly ten years older than me. He is not only older, he is wiser, and yet I sense his deference. He is not intimidated. No, it is more of an appreciation or admiration. I find it surprising.

He is the middle child with two siblings. It would have been a Leave-it-to-Beaver kind of childhood if violence had not been involved. His family was the church-going kind. His dad was even a well-respected Deacon and his mother lovingly and neurotically cared for the children. Thomas was the most frequent target of his father's rage, but it was his mother who on infrequent occasions would suffer the beatings.

His family home was surrounded by open fields, perfect for exploring. When he was eight, the family moved to the suburbs before the developers could dot the hills with track homes. He was a good boy until he was bad. Then he ditched school, got high, rode a motorcycle, and yet still played football. Unlike the other bad boys, he was a love, too.

He planned to marry his high-school sweetheart. She was the one who filled out his college application and she was the reason he went. When she transferred colleges, he followed and spent the second semester living in the girl's dorm. After their relationship ended he left school and traveled the country laying wire for the telephone company, reading books, skiing, and riding his motorcycle. Once he finally went back to school, he followed his bachelor's degree with a masters and promptly enrolled in graduate school to earn his Ph.D. Of course by then he was in love again and married.

Thomas looks nothing like a doctor and exactly like the pirate ancestor in his family. He begins the story, handed down because pirates did not keep journals, of his great-great-great-grandfather, the pirate captain. I sit comfortably in the leather chair, sipping wine and listening attentively to his tale of buried treasure and pirate adventures.

The resemblance is unquestionable. Thomas has a permanent tan. His dark hair is a mere suggestion shaved tightly against a shiny bold dome, and his grin is outlined by a goatee. He runs and lifts weights and I very much appreciate the outcome of so much effort.

He has an imposing presence. People step aside to make room for him whether it is needed or not. He is anti-establishment, obviously. Every inch is raw man, muscular and edged, except for his eyes, which betray his countenance. They are a deep blue, the color of the sea, or a mysterious gray, or a barefoot-through-the-grass-green, and they are always smiling.

His voice is sandy and low and articulates his words courageously. I wait for the moments when he calls me "gorgeous" and "beautiful." If he is the descendant of a pirate, and there is no question from his appearance, then it was not the pillaging and murder that drove his ancestor, instead it was the promise of the coming horizon and a love of the open sea.

WIND, SUNLIGHT, AND A WAVE

It began pretty innocently, though, didn't it? I like to tell myself it did. Except the emails we wrote kept piling up—simple thoughts falling to deeper questions and ideas, and then to yearnings. Weeks passed, then months. Exchanges that made me laugh until I couldn't breathe and at times left me weeping to realize the depth of life's struggle, always forcing me to reevaluate.

I love Josephine's questions, it is clear they protect a tender heart. She is the oldest daughter and the perfect illustration of the role Dr. John Bradshaw describes as the "hero." She was an only child until her brother was born and eight-year-old Josephine forfeited her childhood to play mother.

At sixteen she moved out and left Oliver with their alcoholic mother to save herself. She cries when she shares the pact they had made to stay together and protect each other. Her voice cracks with the heartache it caused when she finally decided to leave. Six years later, in her first year of marriage, she moved her teenage brother two hundred miles and became guardian while Oliver finished high school. During the time Josephine was refusing to see me, she was sharing every detail of her life, her dreams and her wounds.

Looking back, I think those letters and phone calls held some of the most important lessons of my life. This afternoon she called me while I was finishing up some reports. Her current lover is some out-of-state attorney. She tells me everything, in part because she is too self-assured to hide anything and also so she can keep the distance between us. On the drive home from his hotel room, she wants to know how to determine the line between sanity and insanity.

I put away my papers and sit up straight. Whatever answer I give her, she will remember. I want to make sure I get this one right. "Insanity is when a person's actions are destructive to themselves or to the people they care about; they recognize this and yet they continue with the same choices, anyway."

"Oh," she giggles. "Well, no destruction today."

Josephine attracts two types of men. The guarded ones recognize the danger of attaching to her, and it is dangerous. They put up walls to keep themselves safe. Ultimately, she leaves them because they don't offer true intimacy or what she craves most, the opportunity to be vulnerable. The sensitive types want to possess her—they need acceptance, loyalty, or ownership. Josephine leaves them, too, because they are often insecure and dependent.

She is continually searching for a man secure enough to honor her independence and autonomy, and strong enough to cherish and protect her. Her hero comes from a place of strength and has no need to burden her with additional demands. She is looking for an impossible combination, the security where she can finally let go and relax, and an equal challenger where she can explore her own power. The problem with many women today is they unfairly expect men to be heroes then insist they don't need saving. It's no wonder we're confused.

I had no interest in riding the white and shining horse, what I sought was meaning—understanding and awareness. I never wanted to possess Josephine, and I never felt the need to protect myself from her strength or possess her beauty. How can you contain the wind, capture sunlight, or hold a wave? I understood her from the beginning. I just wanted to be near her, the wind in my face, warmed by the sun, skimming the vast ocean.

Of course, like so many others I was drawn into the possibility of what it would be like to make love to her. Still, and this is where the path diverges, I refused to chase the fantasy. I shared a course with Josephine beyond all of the ordinary desires. I was captivated by her. Still, the experience I sought most was the raw human need for connection, a reminder I was still flesh and still bled. My attraction was deeper, more soulful, and what I craved most was simply a closer proximity to the radiance of her light.

I knew in a way I'll never be able to explain, Josephine and I were destined to be together. Whatever time could bring, I had an acute awareness of our absolute fate, as if we'd walked this way before and were merely coming around again. It was all too strong, too ancient, and too real. I would sacrifice everything just to live our promise. If only I had known then what was coming…

CHAPTER FOUR

I could never leave my husband to marry Thomas. The reason is because Thomas licks his fingers when he is eating, instead of using a napkin. Oh, I know what you are thinking, "What a petty explanation for such an important decision." I feel my way through life. All I can offer is the patterns which may be endearing in a lover can be unbearable qualities for a husband.

I am rather practical about matters of love. Vince and I lived together for nearly three years before marriage, long enough for me to assess his behavioral patterns and rule out any incompatibilities. After sixteen anniversaries, I can tell you he does not have a single habit which makes me close my eyes or look away. I like him down to the core of his being, and our lives fit. I know we were meant to be together because it feels like we have been partners for eternity. Occasionally I wish he were more engaged or there was more passion between us. I think he wishes the same from me. Passion is a hard thing to sustain through years of togetherness.

The wonderful thing about having a lover is how he pays attention to your beauty. The wonderful thing about having a husband is how he pays attention to your inadequacies. Between the confidence encouraged by your lover and the clear directives provided by your marital partner, there is unlimited potential for personal development.

Occasionally Thomas and I are swept up in the fantasy of running away together. We have temporary visions of commandeering a sailboat into the sunset. When it comes to marriage, we have both had enough experience to know, deciding which direction to drive is a great deal more exciting than deciding what to do about a broken transmission, refinancing a home, or investing correctly for retirement. There is no greater passion killer than the real life realities of balancing budgets, cleaning the house, scooping dog poop, or determining a path to restorative justice for a child's unfortunate decision.

Thomas and I share a commitment to adventure. Each time we are together feels brand new. Thomas knows I love surprises and new experiences. Since our first date, he never takes me to the same places. His goal has been to spoil me with new sights and sensations. I love him for this and also for something else.

Thomas is rugged. He reminds me of a western cowboy. Today's amenities have softened the American will for survival. Men and women no longer face the concerns over hunting down the day's meal or protecting their families from marauding tribes. For the shrinking middle class, today's shared concern is where to find the nearest Starbucks.

Not Thomas. He makes his own coffee every morning, and it is not the gourmet nonsense everyone is gaga over. He has strong hands calloused over from lifting, building things, and fixing broken stuff and broken people. I feel the hard spots across my skin and I pretend they have emerged from the rough wood of the ship's helm or from pushing a hand plow across a virgin field. Thomas has a masculinity which often eludes the contemporary man.

If Thomas has been angry, it has been concealed from me. He does not even have to raise his voice and people give him whatever he wants. I have no doubts, if his fierceness was to find an escape hatch, he could squash a metropolitan city.

We had lunch this afternoon in a quaint little French restaurant in an outdoor street mall with live performers offering spontaneous entertainment in exchange for tips. Afterward we got stuck in a traffic jam because of road construction. I worried aloud I was going to be late to greet my daughters as they came skipping off the school bus at the end of our cul-de-sac. Thomas got out of the car, walked six car lengths in front, and spoke to a construction worker. Before he even got back into the car the man in the orange vest began moving the traffic cones, opening up a second lane. As the cars began to move forward, I asked, "What did you say?"

Thomas smiled. "I just told him I had to get my girl home."

I appreciate how American women have been liberated. And we have been liberated. We are no longer victims to our gender or slaves to social and political constraints; economic equality remains our last frontier. There is not enough gratitude for the sacrifices my predecessors have made in ensuring opportunity and near-equal rights for women. Equality does not mean gone are the days of chivalry. In my eyes, nothing is more valiant than a man who stands up in defense of a woman, even if he does lick his fingers. Besides, I have watched Thomas approach my lips with similar fervor. I would never dream of taming such savagery.

THE UNSPOKEN CONTRACT

In time, the e-mails turned to discussions over coffee, spontaneous lunches downtown, phone calls to share some simple moment, or just meeting to talk on a park bench and watch the waning sun's reflection on the lake.

If there was a moment, a single picture to capture those early days for me, it is a warm autumn day with Josephine resting her leg against mine as she reads. We are spread under a tree, the smell of dark earth beneath our noses. The rustle of a soft breeze sings in the distance, and the trembling of shadow and light dance in the branches above.

The outside world calls to us and we are oblivious. We lie together and just talk about everything: life, the future, hopes, family, and simple thoughts. We share tearful conversations about marriage, all we aspire for our children, wishful ideas, past hurts, deep yearnings, and all the meaningless shit that still pops up on any given day. We share secrets so deep naked vulnerability passes over us like a warm rain. At times we burst and roar until the tears stream and the air loses itself in heaving gasps. God, how we laugh. We just get it—the ridiculous theater of everyday life and the simple embrace of the irony in all things.

I've made my living reading people and for the longest time, I thought I couldn't read Josephine, then I understood. There isn't anything to interpret because she doesn't hide anything. If she thinks it, or feels it, she says it. She isn't making any demands or passing any judgement, she's simply providing information, so each person can make the appropriate decisions. I find it refreshing and sometimes hilarious; others often find her style of direct communication scary as hell. She finds that entertaining.

This woman has an enormous range. Her ability to connect people to meaning is unparalleled. She leads with both command and compassion. Her audience trusts everything she says, and they should.

I am the privileged receiver of an entirely different side of Josephine. The part only revealed when she feels perfectly safe, the side that is child-like and silly. She chooses me as her playmate and it thrills me to see her delight in the simplest things: furry caterpillars, homemade ice cream, and a budding flower. Never have I witnessed such an open and generous heart. She's made a pact with innocence. She adores animals, children, and elderly people—there's a luminous exchange, a mystical alchemy that occurs through their interactions.

I sit on the blanket next to her while she chatters on about the characters in her book. Then she stops mid-sentence and asks, "How would you like to die?"

It's a question I've never considered and immediately I realize the answer. She replies eagerly, "Don't tell me...let me guess."

Each guess is so far-fetched and elaborate I can't stop laughing. Then I ask her, "How would you like to die?"

"I've known the answer to this question for a long-time," she smiles. "I've even pictured it. I'm an old woman, tiny and shrunk with a great posture because of all of the Yoga I've done. I still have my teeth, a yellowish hue, but the majority are still there. My hair is silvery gray and my skin is thin and wrinkled. I'm sitting comfortably on a chair in the sun while little children play all around me. They run up and tell me their secrets and show me their treasures. I praise them and celebrate their discoveries. It's so beautiful, the trees are blooming and the grass is green. Everywhere there are these wonderful little children of different ages, different colors and even different abilities. I'm right there with them amidst their joy and curiosity until I take my last breath.

She looks at me squarely and grinning and concludes, "I intend to die on an inhale."

Her subtle kiss grazes my cheek as I feel the release of my own frustration and past resentments. It was enough. It was. In the moment I reach for her hand and feel her take mine and something shifts. A willingness to accept—a quiet yielding to life with all of its surprises.

CHAPTER FIVE

When the ego has been untethered from the human psyche, power struggles disappear, threats go unrecognized, and scarcity exists no more. My ego makes an occasional visit, however, we had our big farewell ceremony some time ago. I thanked my ego for keeping me safe and protected all of those years during a treacherous childhood.

The philosophers and psychologists often refer to the ego in the negative. My ego was stellar. I was really blessed to have a lunatic mother and unconscious father. Together they presented the perfect opportunity for self-actualization. During the reign of my ego, I learned the following valuable lessons:

You can't trust anyone.
The world is a scary place.
You are all alone.
You are not safe.

Thanks to good old Mom and Dad, and I mean this lovingly, all of those lessons were true in my youth. My friend, the ego, pulled me through the long crisis and quite possibly saved my life. Thomas also had a shitty childhood, only he had a lunatic father and an unconscious mother, dolloped with a topping of sexual abuse by the church's youth leader. When your parents are whack jobs, you have a tendency to hurry and figure out "who you are" in a sincere hope you will not turn out resembling either, meaning crazy or numb.

It is unfortunate so many tortured children grow up and become their parents. In my case and Thomas's, too, rebellion and an army of healers salvaged the wreckage (provided we keep the alcohol at a minimum and completely avoid cocaine, crystal meth, and cough syrup).

Contrary to the self-help books, religious zealots, and Grandmother's advice, although she is normally the most credible source of wisdom, there is no final destination. I try and break through the distortions and live in the moment, more and more it is all beginning to feel like a dream. Sometimes I think Thomas is a splendid illusion, other times his hand on the small of my back feels like the only real thing. Both are true.

There is a reason the cosmos drew Thomas and me together. Only we probably will not see the reason until the relationship is over, if even then. Fortunately much of our healing had begun long before our merger, and we escaped the traditional neurotic dependency binding so many of today's couples—you know, the ones who keep trying to close the hole inside them by stuffing in another person. Only instead of filling one hole they end up with two holes.

Finding acceptance with my parents and disconnecting from the ego have brought me quite close to a state of detachment. Also, I think my soul's been around long enough to recognize the temporal nature of life and it steers clear of expectation and entitlement. I have spent many occasions apologizing for my detachment until recently when I read a book on Buddhism. Spiritual yogis experience complete detachment of things, people, and outcomes. Now I can stop questioning the line between mental illness and spirituality.

My contract with Vince, whatever it is, must be etched in gold letters and carved in marble.

Over the years I have learned to greet the people who come into my life as teacher or healer. Sometimes I play one of those roles for them. I wonder about the specifics of my contract with Thomas. I only know we are bound to one another. I wonder if a completed contract will mark the end of our beautiful journey. I worry, too, while Thomas is teaching me the difference between reality and illusion, in the end I will provide him with my usual lessons in detachment.

TOO MUCH LOVE

Oh, but I don't want to mislead. If only it were all so perfect and without complication. If only the answers were so easily conceived by something as simple as falling in love. If only...

Here again.

I will forever yield to Josephine's hurried call—any fleeting chance to connect. Pull anchor and reset course on a moment's notice, to another deserted parking lot between my home and hers. The drive is rushed, the anticipation a heroin-racing surge of adrenaline. I think, "It's only been a couple of days, for Christ sake." I can't take my foot off the gas, certainly not for something as trivial as a yellow light bleeding into red. When I arrive, I have to remind myself the whole purpose is to relax together. "Fucking calm down. It's not life or death." Or is it?

Pulling into the parking spot, I feel my breath returning slowly...slowly. As the view of the stoplight comes into focus, I watch the turn, inspect each passing car. The seconds pass. There's a more subtle stab of want, waiting for her touch, her scent. I change the radio and check my phone. My eyes close only to be haunted by her smile. I take a breath, hit the radio dial again, and look out over the dark field, recalling the path leading me here.

All of the stolen moments, weak attempts to stave off the inevitable, the insatiable tyrant of desire: her small hand curled in my palm; the drives through the country with no destination; an unexpected call; napping in the middle of the day; songs that became ours; the irresistible zest of pineapple; a late check-in when she's out with the girls; her hand grazing my thigh; long emails and love letters; a spontaneous meeting at some dive; her joy in sharing a tended garden.

Shivering, I return suddenly chilled by the night air. Headlights pass out on the corner. The music plays and I force myself to take a long breath. I pull my fleece from the back seat as winter points her gnarled finger outside the car window.

Then a flash of light and she turns into the lot. Called again to the night, every desire returns to me in an instant. I feel her closeness like a storm of rage and fire. She'll park beside me and rip open my heart again with a simple nod, that sly grin. I'll yield gratefully to the pain of too much love, and then slide my seat back to grant her sanctuary. By the time she opens the door I'm already consumed.

Resting against the window and flashing those impossible eyes. I touch her cheek. I run a finger across her lip and open her mouth with my thumb before kissing her. My fingers trace the lines of her tight jeans and I grab her hips to pull her closer. I want to memorize her for the times we are apart. I touch the small of her back, her round ass, and each curve—every nuance of her being. I brush her curls aside and bury my hold into her mane, touching her mouth against mine, the sweet enraptured craving of her tongue. I am amazed to discover she is here, in my lap again. We are far beyond the clawing demands of this world or the clamoring horde waiting in the darkness just outside these doors.

She looks me straight-on and coos, "You know you are going to fall in love with me."

I smile a confident cock-sure smile, while my tone betrays me, "Is that right?"

Her warning has come too late.

CHAPTER SIX

Love, while magical, is most certainly overdone in the literary world. Ours is a story of surrender, mine, his, and ours. Thomas courted me for nearly a year before our first kiss. It was another nine months before we made love.

Our first time was not memorable. Thomas, I am certain, would prefer to completely forget. For me, though, our first sexual experience clarified our relationship, this was not a simple union of lust.

The first time he entered me, we had met at his office. The sexual tension between us had been drawn out beyond the point of exhaustion.

I finally gave into him for reasons which exceed normal patterns of reason. If you must know, I wanted it over. Thoughts of Thomas and whether to make love or abstain consumed me. The physical part, or lack thereof, was bearable. The emotional part, however, began interfering in every thought and invading every aspect of living. We were spending a lot of time together and it was beginning to take from my family and work. Even when we were not together Thomas would creep into my thoughts, wake me in my sleep, and hold me hostage to my fantasies. I wanted my head back and I fully expected, based on previous relationships, by giving him my body, my mind would again be liberated.

I do not know how our beliefs take root or even where they stem. Perhaps it was those earlier messages my mother passed on from her mother, "If you have sex with a man before he has made the commitment to marry you, he will leave you. While this has never been the case, those childhood warnings are hard to shake. The idea I was some conquest for Thomas and he would move on to the next challenge as soon as he bedded me did not fit, but I still hoped finally making love would represent some sort of trophy allowing both of us to move forward and away.

My thinking may also have stemmed from my experiences of abandonment. My father had left six times during the course of my parent's eighteen-year marriage. Either way, I felt Thomas's grip tightening around me and I was searching for a way to break free. It is hard to understand how making love to someone could be equated with severing a connection, the human species is a fucked-up lot, and I do not profess to be any better.

Our first sexual encounter together was not an instance of intolerable passion, rather an attempt to escape the spell cast over me. I see it now as a battle to be free, the last stand for Josephine Island. Eventually I lost, of course. That is the secret of divinity. Divinity is not realized through a victory, it is actualized in our surrender.

In his corner office with papers strewn everywhere and a phone ringing nearby, I attempted to guide Thomas near my coveted temple. Intuitively he must have understood I wanted his body as a farewell gift. At first he would not harden, resisting my offer and our finality. I kissed his neck, unzipped his pants, and began stroking him. I saw the look in his eyes, hesitation. I whispered, "I cannot wait a moment longer, please Thomas."

He dropped my skirt to the floor and bent me over face down on his polished glass desk arching my hips towards him. He brought himself forward to meet me, parting the tenderness between my thighs. Briefly I felt the strength of his hands wrap around the outside of my hips and pull me toward him. Then he came. Within seconds it was over.

Thomas was embarrassed. He tried to explain or apologize; the details are not what I remember. For me it was the disappointment I had hoped to set me free. Days later I still could not shake him from my thoughts. I would hear his voice in the wind and see his eyes in every shade of blue. As hard as I tried, I could not rid my mind of Thomas. A week later we tried making love again. He wanted redemption. Again I demanded my release.

After a romantic dinner, a bottle of wine, and the privacy of a hotel room, a similar experience was repeated. This time, despite my coaxing, he could not sustain an erection. The look in his eyes this time was fear. He left the room abruptly and I sat on the edge of the bed exposed and wondering if he would ever come back. By the time I had dressed, he returned. He packed up our belongings and we left the room without speaking. He called me the next morning with rationalizations and more apologies. I could not hear his words.

Thomas vacillated between frustration and sadness, but I knew it was I who had been defeated. The debacle of our lovemaking was not enough to deter me from this man. Our bond exceeded the emotional, mental, and physical states of being. It was clear to me, my body would not satiate what a soul craves. It was then I began to understand no matter what I gave or withheld, I would not be liberated from Thomas.

It is far more than sexual desire. Here is the man who holds the map to my buried desires, and carried the ladder reaching beyond my fortified defenses. In him I hear the beckoning of spirit whispering to me softly, "Come into the light. You, the island, are not separate, you are one with me."

THE HEART OF IT ALL

Josephine…my ruin and my salvation. For months, no years, I had imagined the moment I would finally have her. I could close my eyes and visualize every detail of her skin, every line of her body. I had imagined making love to her so many times the tastes and smells overpowered reality.

When she finally offered herself to me, I was stunned cold. It's a ridiculous dichotomy now of course, as if touching, and kissing, and sharing your innermost thoughts wouldn't lead to the consummation of those desires. I remember thinking, "We simply can't go here, because this is a place I can't come back from." I had my princess wife, and my perfect job, and my beautiful boys. I had to be able to return home.

In my head, I had talked myself out of intercourse, just so I could endure the nearness of the essence that is Josephine. The truth is, I was madly in love with her from the beginning. From the moment we met I knew there was no one like her, and never would be again. And here she is wet and alive and bent over begging for me to take her. I couldn't believe it. There would be no turning back from here for me—not a chance. A million questions raced and I knew everything was about to change. Could I ever be enough? Would the realness I felt for her ever live up to the dream? And, for God sakes, what happens now?

After all, this wasn't going to be some pink panty fling where you get off and walk away. This was Josephine; everything means something here. I remember thinking, "I can't fuck this up by being too rough, or too gentle, or too clumsy." This moment had to be perfect, just the way I have always imagined, just the way she has imagined.

It was disastrous, a thundering cacophony of guilt and desire running headlong through my veins along with a desperate need to fulfill her in every way. My head was pounding with all of the pent-up moments and unnamed yearnings which had brought us to this critical point. It was too much, way too much.

CHAPTER SEVEN

I remember the first moment I fell in love with him. Not the first moment I loved him, the first moment I became his.

Months had passed since the first failed attempts at lovemaking. It was now late in the spring, the two year anniversary of his initial email. Vince was again in New York on business. My two girls were invited to sleepovers. Initially Thomas was away, too, visiting a sick friend. Upon hearing of my availability, he created his own.

We met at a hotel on the northern most border of the city. An area unfamiliar to us both and offering some degree of anonymity and escape from the other life we both knew and loved. It would be our first complete night together. Our clothes were off within seconds of the door closing. It was the only time I remember feeling afraid with him. It was as if I knew this one event would transform my white picket fence reality.

Room service was ordered from the steak house across the street. We took turns feeding each other bites of filet mignon, asparagus tips, baked potato with melted butter and sour cream. With the plates cleared, we copulate again, the rough kind where you lash about turning this way, angling that way. Two lovers' exasperated attempts to finally get enough of the other, a known impossibility. My body succumbs beneath him, over him, until lying next to him I fall asleep breathless and exhausted.

In the middle of the night, I awake. Disoriented by the strange surroundings I search for Thomas's body next to mine. Instantly I am aware of his absence. My eyes, still blurry with sleep, recognize his silhouette draped in a bathrobe and positioned over the small hotel desk. He is only eight feet away, sitting with his back to me as he prepares an evaluation for an upcoming trial. I feel the distance in my bones. I hear the space between us. When I called out for him, the shape it takes in my vocal cords is a cry.

There is a moment between sleep and awake, right before logic enters the mind and emotion runs away with your heart, it is the briefest moment when the soul speaks unencumbered. I did not want to love him. I did not want to hurt anyone.

Hearing my cry, he comes right to me. Sensing my panic, he slips one arm underneath my head and smooths my hair away from my face, tenderly kissing my neck and whispering reassurances. The other arm he wraps over me and around my hip to the opposite thigh. When he brings my naked body to rest against him, he unintentionally slips inside of me. The movement was so subtle, so exquisite.

I discover then, making loving has very little to do with your sexual organs. Making love is a dance of hurts and dreams and the hopeful promise your lover will soothe and deliver.

In the morning Thomas showers behind the glass panels. He leaves the bathroom door ajar. I watch as he steps under the water. I watch him pick up the soap, rub his hands together, and spread the lather over his chest and under each arm. I watch him wash his calves, around his thighs and above. I watch as he lathers the soap in his hands and runs his palms over his head and face. I want to see clearly and completely the man who soothes and delivers.

THE NOT SO GRAND AND NOT SO FINALE

Josephine and I always knew our choices would be interpreted strongly, disdainfully and with immense personal harm. We had compromised our promises. Despite the depth and beauty there would be no offer of redemption. Selfishness, we knew all too well and the consequence of our choices—well, they were inescapable. I wish there had been a way to protect everyone, there simply wasn't. It was a train I couldn't stop. A beautiful tragedy I couldn't explain or make right. It is the course I chose and the one I accept.

From the beginning, Josephine and I confided details about our families and our spouses. What we shared was with a deep respect and love for the lives we had created, always supporting the importance of those ties. It wouldn't be viewed this way. It just couldn't. And I could no more justify those two separate worlds, than to try to explain Daoism to a Christian.

I could argue how we never intended to injure anyone, a trite consolation to all those who would so deeply feel the pain. In the end, there was just no way to mend the two. Marriage is marriage, and affairs are what they are, potentially exhilarating and most certainly ugly.

We both understood our responsibility. We also felt irresistibly drawn to each other on an inexplicable soulful level. We more than understood the cost to our families. Still, there was no acceptable way to steer the course. And so we danced by the red hot fire until one simple event.

A night, never to be forgotten.

All of the tender moments happened, as they had so many times before. Josephine in my lap, resting in the front seat with the radio playing softly. It was another stolen connection in another deserted parking lot. The hour seemed so timeless to me, maybe they all did. Her chestnut eyes, her tender mouth, her head finding safety and rest against my chest. Still knowing into this Eden, change was in the air.

The October pageant was upon us. In our small suburban town, family returns to remember. Yes, for the turkey bearing holidays and to repair separations, more for the simple traditions. These are the small celebrations reminding us of the value of all things true: life, connection, childhood, family, laughter, and simplicity, too often forgotten in the trivialities of life and striving to be remembered. It was the time of harvest and plenty. For the innocent, the carnival, the tiny draped lights and gypsy rides, the smell of caramel popcorn, and the inspired carving of the perfect jack-o-lantern.

We'd be there, all of us: my wife, my in-laws, and our precious children. We gathered to rebirth the tradition I'd known long before I could appreciate the importance of honoring time or season.

I knew Josephine would be there as well. We discussed the circumstances only hours earlier. We considered the option of one of us not going. It had been nearly three years since the holiday party where I sat in the corner and watched her. The relationship had developed slowly, the past nine months had been too rich with intimate adventures and soulful lovemaking. Together we could imagine a future, still there was no escaping reality. The course was too fraught with homes and marriages, families, and most importantly, our children.

Part of me wanted to stay away from the fall festival completely. Vince was traveling and Josephine would be there alone with her daughters, who I knew looked forward to the festival every year. I was desperate to avoid an encounter and yet here we were. The grandparents were arriving, the plans set and my sons bursting with enthusiasm and expectation.

Without question our greatest dreams must be the delicate experiences and youthful wishes of our children; the celebration of their beginning journey and their untarnished discoveries into the world.

The moment is staccato shrill, people streaming about the tent vendors and games of chance. Where did they come from? Impossible—there are too many bodies to represent this old town ablaze with sudden importance. I reach for my sons' tender hands and guide them through the flashing maze of the crowd and the blaring music. Their eyes dart to and fro trying desperately to take it in. You know what's in their heart and it fills you. You've lived it once upon a time in your own distant past.

While stepping into the crowd and guiding them to the next adventure, I see her. Radiant Josephine, framed by her own children holding tightly to their mother's hand. I'd known, of course. We'd already measured it and I tried; goddamn how I tried to anticipate and prepare for the time when our separate worlds would collide against the imaginary world we had built together.

I saw her turn. I watched her head tilt and her eyes smile in recognition. I felt the flutter of all we had experienced and all we had risked. How I wanted to pull her into me, safe from all of the realities of the moment. She and my wife embraced. She reached out a hand to my in-laws, and before they all turned to find me, I slipped into the clamor of the crowd. Concealed within the mass of chatter and prattle, I heard nothing, nothing at all.

Buried amid the crowd, I tried to conceive how I had done the unthinkable. I let go. In a heartless panic, I had just released the tender hands of my boys and walked away. I knew the family surrounded the frail hearts I had yielded and they were quite protected. Still I felt sick to my stomach; in one single moment I was marked with all of the incalculable losses about to come. I could not face the very scene I had painted with my own hands. I began to see clearly what I had become…

The cataclysmic explosion of our worlds treading into each other was unbearable to face for both of us. That night she left only a short voice message. "Thomas, I cannot reconcile this betrayal with my conscience. I love you and I am saying good-bye."

CHAPTER EIGHT

Thomas and I have not spoken in over two weeks. Seeing his wife and sons was sobering. I have endured betrayal. There was a time, many years earlier, before we had children when I thought I might lose Vince.

It was the year before my first daughter was born, a summer when I was both distracted and preoccupied with social and professional interests. Sometimes Vince joined me, and there were often times I went out alone. Without any sort of intention, we began to move in separate directions. Eventually he found emotional support from another woman.

The whole thing was over before their relationship was consummated. The discovery was made early and quickly followed by marriage counseling. The experience challenged us both to once again choose whether to stay in the relationship or head off in different directions. Although eventually we recommitted ourselves to the marriage, there were two weeks in between when choices were being sorted and the future was for a brief moment...undecided. It was a terrifying time for me. I lost eight pounds, took up smoking from my early college years and barely slept. I could not imagine life without Vince. We share a powerful bond.

I knew Sarah did not deserve the agony of a betrayal. I thought of Thomas's boys, too. My whole life has been about healing and teaching. I did not want to be someone else's disease and I did not want to be the instructor on loss and betrayal.

Eventually I had planned for my relationship with Thomas to come to an end anyway. Secret love affairs always lose their sparkle. Someday soon my pirate lover would look older to me: heavy, wrinkled, gray. Even the deep blue of his eyes would appear dulled. His voice would not soothe me, nor would I crave his calloused hands against my skin.

With all of my lovers I ultimately lose interest. My spirit craves adventure. Once I get to know a man intimately and thoroughly, he becomes much less exciting. Over the years I have come to understand this about myself. As a courtesy, I always offer this disclaimer at the start of any new love affair.

Men love this about me. They are competitive in nature so when a woman says, "Don't get attached," or "I'm not available," all they hear is "Catch me if you can." I already know the outcome: heavy, wrinkled, gray. I am honest; still, I try not to extinguish their joy in the chase.

There is a reason I am guarded, an explanation for why I am both protected and removed. Of course all stories lead back to our mothers. Mine is a raging alcoholic and beyond critical, she was cruel. She told so many lies you had to pay very close attention to find any element of truth. Evenings would be particularly difficult. She often hurled insults and called me names...terrible things not worth repeating.

I developed my own bedtime ritual. I would tuck my covers snug between the mattress and the box springs and I would squeeze in from the top so I would be tucked in so tightly I could barely move. It felt like a hug. In the safety of those covers I would rewrite the script. "You are beautiful, Josephine," "You are precious," and "I love you so much." I would recite these and similar phrases until I fell asleep refusing to accept any other reality than the one I created.

Therapists have asked how I learned a conscious practice of self-talk as a young child. I do not know the answer. My best guess is from the beginning I knew fear had a deadening effect on life. I have a lot of practice rejecting the things that frighten me.

SEPARATE SLEEPING QUARTERS

Sarah and I don't share a bed. It's been that way for at least a decade. The original excuse began with my snoring, rather than the truth. Not that tens of thousands of women don't weather this long-suffering irritation every night. I get it. It's just for us, the marital issues which led to sleeping on the couch in the basement every night were so much deeper. Two surgeries and all the sleep studies and devices couldn't really address the more blaring issues concerning intimacy.

In time we grew to have the typical dysfunctional American marriage. Whenever it came to our sons, household chores, and paying bills, we could get the job done. Courtship and the grand wedding were followed by building a home, the children, renovations, and a second mortgage. There are the promises of more opportunity with higher education, followed by excessive student loans. Next come the bigger house, the needed renovations, the newer cars, the kids' expenses, the unfathomable insurance costs, the medical bills and debt, and debt, and debt.

Maybe I could have weathered all of the challenges, maybe. I certainly loved Sarah. Still shouldering all of the weight ALONE without a lover or a friend. Without someone capable of sharing the storm with me: taking my hand; whispering in my ear; telling me I was desirable or allowing me to touch her late at night. If you brush my hand aside whenever I try to touch you, complain you're too tired, have a headache, are on your period, or there are children in the house, eventually, I won't bother you.

In the end it all has nothing to do with the Great American Dream. It is all…it must be…about feeling connected. The houses, cars, bank accounts, professions, degrees, debts, businesses—it all means nothing in the end without a true partner to share the obstacles and the rewards.

I'm not blaming Sarah. I was not a true partner. Step by step, gradually, I became the most prodigious liar imaginable. It started with my first email to Josephine. It wafted in the air of every early phone conversation. It was consecrated in our very first kiss. It was the consequence of every touch, every time I pulled her into me, every moment we laughed together and every night I lay alone and fantasized about being near her.

I was burning my own sense of integrity like a wildfire while I staved off the costs in my head. And even then, I couldn't let go. Josephine was my connection to everything beautiful. I willfully walked into the inconceivable role of deceiver.

I could say, I was protecting Sarah. I certainly tried. I could say, I wanted to protect the children from the coming storm, this would be true also. What I couldn't outrun were my own lies, and especially the sense I was really only trying to protect myself.

I knew the cost and the losses would be catastrophic. Families were going to be torn apart. Traditions were going to come to an end. Relationships with family, friends, and neighbors were going to be destroyed. If Josephine and I continue, our other worlds would eventually be changed forever.

CHAPTER NINE

You may think my choices do not honor my husband. Perhaps at times you are right. I do love him. I wish I could be all things. I wish my own feet would not dance in other meadows, so happily. It is not to be. At the end of the day, I simply cannot give myself to Vince without honoring who it is I have to give.

He honors me, too. From the beginning Vince has accepted my need for freedom and adventure along with my definition of loyalty. He knows about Thomas and the others before him, although I spare him the details. About ten years into our relationship, we decided to open our marriage. This meant being honest and safe and not monogamous.

Some people term our agreement polygamous. We have never liked labels and have yet to identify with any one specific community. Our arrangement is to simply remove any barriers or limitations restricting us from connecting with others, including spiritually and sexually. As human beings, we are designed to connect to one another. My husband is free to share himself and pursue other women wherever the connection may lead. I honor his freedom equally.

Vince is handsome, brilliant, funny, and kind. Women often throw themselves at him. He rarely shows any interest, and it is even rarer when he chooses sexual intimacy. The chosen few are always much younger. Mid-twenties is the standard, with personalities to match their perky breasts. Vince is far more emotional than I, and he takes a long time getting to know a woman. Ironically, by the time he pulls back the deeper layers, he has usually lost interest.

We have always spoken openly and honestly about our relationships. Of course, I ask a lot of questions. Sometimes I ask for reassurances. Until Thomas, those reassurances came more readily. Aside from the one day a week and an occasional evening when no one is around to notice, I am fully present for my husband and my children.

On the other six days of the week, their joys, their comfort take precedence over all else. Schedules revolve around their needs. I sneak my work into the hours when my children are at school and Vince is at work. Otherwise dinner is on the table at 6:30 p.m., the house is tidy and comfortable, children are picked up and delivered, clean laundry is waiting in their bins to be folded and put away, the social calendar is full, and the gardens are abundant with vegetables, herbs, and flowers.

I am a master at compartmentalization. When I am with Vince, I am his alone. He gets frustrated occasionally and creates distance between us when he feels the need to protect himself or resentment sneaks in, other times he is content to share me and bask in my happiness regardless of its origin.

There is one part I do not share with anyone else besides my husband. It is my promise to stay. I see Vince exactly as he is and I accept him completely. If his eyes lose their color, I do not notice, my pledge to stand beside him is too strong.

It is Saturday morning again in a distant hotel. Thomas and I have made love four times between the hours of 11 p.m. and 8 a.m. I love make-up sex! I woke huddled under his shoulder with the smell of him in every inhale and the strength of his chest shielding me from a distant reality. At first I lay there questioning whether I should wake him or not. I watched for any signs of consciousness.

Patience is not my virtue, and so I tenderly reached for him and then the swelling in my hand as he murmured, "No! No!" punctuated with a smile. I climbed on top of him, my breasts pressing into his chest. I whispered, "Shhh, baby, you don't even have to open your eyes. I'm going to do all the work. You lay very still, my love, and pretend this is only a dream."

Then my hand directs him sleepily inside of me.

Lying face-to-face afterward and feeling so very proud of myself, Thomas whispers, "Can I tell you a secret?"

"Yes," because secrets right after surprises are my very favorite.

"You ordered the number one last night."

"What?"

The night before we ate dinner at a Greek restaurant called The Athenian. When the server set down our plates, I said, "Oh, this isn't what I ordered. I requested the special."

"I'll be right back," the server said, returning seconds later with the waitress who had taken the order. She said politely, "You closed the menu and ordered the number one."

I remember looking at Thomas, his expression neutral, eyes always smiling. "Maybe lamb sounds like 'one,' but I do recall ordering the special."

"I'll have the kitchen make the special right up for you," the waitress offered quickly, taking the number one with her.

Thomas pushed his plate forward indicating he would wait. "No, please, I don't want your food to get cold and I am still finishing my salad."

Then I asked, "Did you hear me order the special?"

And taking a bite of food, he nodded, still smiling.

So here we are the next morning and the secret he is whispering in my ear illuminates a small error in my righteousness. "Why didn't you say something? I asked you."

"You wanted the special."

"I know." I winced. "But it would have been more important to me to recognize my mistake than to get what I wanted." Then covering my eyes with my hands, I added, "What were you thinking when I was telling the waitress she had gotten the order wrong?"

Pulling me close to him and looking directly into me, "I was thinking to the waitress, 'Don't dicker over what she said and what she thought she said. If my baby wants the special, then make sure she gets the special.'"

Yep, it is quite simple, really: women just want to eat, sleep, and have sex, and they want a man that makes those the easiest and most fun!

VULNERABILITY

From the beginning, our love affair held all of the promise and anticipation of a grand adventure. For us, there is no charted course and there never was. It all happens in the moment, wherever the journey may lead.

On the days we're together, anything, absolutely anything, can happen. Plans are sketchy at best with the acknowledgment life is never static. The joy has always been in the risk and discovery of wherever the path leads. A course so easily turned by the simplest of cues. Is the day warm or overcast? Am I feeling strong or weak? Do I seek the comfort of a dark room or the vastness of the open horizon? Am I drawn to the familiar or the unknown? Do I yearn for deep intimacy, thundering sexual release, or just some good conversation?

Most amazing is how often we're on the same page, how effortlessly we seem to read the moment together and connect before yielding to the day. Such undefined resonance and acceptance of desire, wherever it leads.

And if only it were this simple; life still intercedes with regularity, always shocking in its insistence returning us back into the world we once knew.

Josephine schedules her foot surgery during a given day. Vince has an important meeting and she asks me to accompany her. I arrive early. The drive to the hospital is quiet, the waiting area hushed like a library. When she's called, I instinctively rise before the attending nurse waves me back down. A short time later, shielded by the surgical curtains, I stroke her hand and watch her eyes as the drug's effects take hold. I make up stories and jokes to relieve the tension.

A bustling nurse flitters in and in her duties observes how we touch each other. She asks how long we've been married, and Josephine laughs and winks at me. Then too quickly it's time to leave. I kiss her softly on the forehead. I want so badly to protect her. Instead, I pace over and over against the walls of the televised waiting room, meaningless Hollywood gossip without any redeeming hope of depth or truth. I'm irritated.

Thankfully, it is not a long respite before the surgeon rescues me with his report. Just a simple procedure, I realize it was impossible to stop holding my breath. By the time they allow me to return to my lover's side, I'm crazy with the need to touch her. The nurse offers a minute of assurance before blankly reading off each unlikely outcome or possible failure. I nod without hearing. I just watch Josephine's eyes, always her eyes; massaging her thigh as I have so many times before. They need me to sign some form. I'm not authorized, I scratch my signature on the form. I just want to return her safely home.

She feels so fragile today. Shouldering her on her one good leg to the couch I experience again the surprising sense of honor and devotion—her place of strength, her refuge. I find myself filled with immeasurable gratitude, graced with her trust and her unconditional love. So I gather her blankets and fix her tea. I prepare the ice packs. I deliver a plate of saltine crackers and Sprite to counter the effects of the anesthesia. I rest her head in my lap, stroke her hair, and urge her to rest.

It all seems so effortless and simple, so natural. Until the phone rings with a shrill. Her husband is pulling into the driveway just outside. The garage door climbs upward, mechanical grating in my ears. He's all too aware of my car on the curb. He knows. There's a quick, unseen acknowledgment as he reverses course and spins the tires, the screech—a terse scolding to the unfaithful and a wounded cry from the betrayed.

I close my eyes, breath caught, words failing. Too quickly, the realities of our other lives explode back into focus. This is not my place. I'm still just an illusion, driven with immediate, shattering clarity back to my place upon the silent, invisible throne. I am forced to remember: Josephine doesn't belong to me. She never has. She doesn't belong to him, either.

We are alone, all of us.

Alone. Together.

CHAPTER TEN

My relationship with Thomas has moved incredibly slowly, largely in part to our family and marital obligations. I also have to thank Thomas, who is so cool and collected; time does not exist in his world. He is only nine years older and a tad wiser. There is a certainty about him which steadies those around him. Also, he asks for nothing and expects nothing from me. I have been able to grow into our love naturally and in my own way, which is to admit, I have resisted more than anything.

My fears are many: I do not want to hurt our children or our spouses; I do not want to disrupt the lives we have created for ourselves; I do not want to be faced with difficult decisions; I do not want to lose myself to this powerful, beautiful man, who looks at me and touches me in a way that leaves me sometimes questioning...everything.

It was in the third year of our love affair before we took a vacation together and stepped away from the familiar securities. We loaded our belongings and drove to the coast for two nights. Thomas has an uncle with a beach cottage. From a distance, it is right out of a dream. A perfectly square white clapboard house with peeling paint and a porch with wide stairs and a spindled railing. Upon entering the house I could see the Feng is totally off from the Shui.

All the furniture is pushed up against the outer walls. Not that anyone would want to utilize it anyway. Nothing is coordinated and the motif, if there were one, meanders between western and nursing home. Did I mention this was a beach house? The kitchen table, plastic with three white chairs, the only pieces of matching furniture and still uncoordinated. The sofa was a sharp contrast in cold black leather.

Since I am being honest, I am kind of fanatical about textures and taste. I give a lot of attention to food, music, art, and the overall sensory experience. It is kind of like my spiritual practice since eating, resting and moving are the essentials of our human existence. Do not misunderstand, I know the people in our lives and relationships are paramount to room décor or a four-course meal. I put more consideration into cooking for others than I do myself. And I would much rather experience Egyptian cotton sheets with high thread counts in the arms of a lover than sleeping all alone. Music, I'll take any time.

Outside the beach cottage was beautiful, inside it was disquieting. I knew it would be difficult to restrain myself from moving furniture or consulting paint swatches so I settled myself outside on the porch with a blanket I had brought from home, a glass of pinot noir, and a Toni Morrison novel.

Thomas moves soundlessly. Quiet and alone are ordinarily the necessary conditions for my preferred state of solitude. Thomas is the exception, when we are together I want to feel his skin against me, hear the rhythm of his voice. I motion for him to lie with me in the hammock. He raises his eyebrows acquiescing. It is an awkward fit, the two of us sandwiched together. Neither of us complains, happy to be alone in the stillness.

In the late afternoon we take a walk along the ridge and peak in the windows of vacated summer homes. Farther on down the beach I find the perfect seaside cottage. The back door is unlocked, the day's miracle. Inside are wooden floors, large windows darned with white linen curtains. It is incredibly small and simple, probably less than 600 square feet. Two bedrooms are set in each corner, one has a queen-size bed and down quilt, the second bedroom has two twin beds separated by an antique bureau. The kitchen has one counter with a porcelain sink and wood-burning stove converted to gas. The kitchen table is placed under a window looking out on the ocean with four simple wooden chairs all harmonized, none of them matching.

The fireplace, handcrafted out of large stones is encircled with a petite love seat, two comfortable chairs. Behind the sitting area is a small game table framed by two chairs and another window. Near the back door is a wet room. Beyond the doorway, the sink basin, the shoe cubby, and coat racks, is a cozy window seat set off in a nook with a complete view of the beach. When I close my eyes, I can still see the cottage perfectly.

Three days is the longest stretch of time Thomas and I have been together. During the silence of the porch, along those walks on the beach, and in the strength of his arms I did what I feared most, I began to lose myself.

When our last evening arrived, Thomas, sensing my dislike of the interior cottage, carries our dinner to the picnic table in the sand. My pirate lover cracks open the fresh oysters we picked up on the drive in from the local fish market.

If I have any insecurity, it can be found in my cooking. I hate serving anything less than a perfect meal. My problem is I am usually multitasking and occasionally my meals are compromised in the process. Tonight I overcook the tuna steaks. I set the seared tuna steaks with a reduction of wasabi, soy sauce, and a hint of fresh ginger on top of a mound of citrus greens and Quinoa and hope Thomas won't notice.

Instead of appreciating the setting sun on the horizon and the gentle rise on the ocean's waves, I watch Thomas chew. He simply smiles back at me. Finally I break down and confess my grilling mistake. His response is to burst out laughing.

When he finally recovers, he patiently takes his last bite, wipes his mouth grinning broadly, and picks me up over his shoulder. Thomas carries me closer to the water and drops me tenderly on a nest of blankets concealed by a sand bluff. Then he tosses a match igniting a blaze of firewood. While he undresses me, all I can think of is the cottage and what it would be like to spend every day like this here with Thomas and our barefoot children covered in sand and tanned by the sun.

My pirate captain moves his hands slowly across my every curve and around every corner for what feels like hours. He touches every part of me, my cheek, lips, and neck, neglecting nothing. He watches the most vulnerable part of me, my stomach, relax beneath his palm. His hands are large and they cover the complete distance of my body gracefully. Around my waist, over my backside, along my thighs, past my knees, encompassing my feet, his hands follow my body appreciatively, again and again.

The ocean courses and the waves slap against the shore. I can see the flames of the fire reflected in his blue eyes. Something far back remembers infancy and what it felt like to be so loved, so protected and so completely nurtured. When we release ourselves to the pleasure place, I feel the wet tears upon my cheeks and wonder if they are mine.

THE AMERICAN DREAM

The thing about marriage is it's so fucking predictable. After 20 years, I've gotta say...I really just don't understand the grand tortured emphasis of our society on the unquestioned sanctity of marital unions. We fall in love at an age where the need to settle in and establish roots holds every appeal, and we so willingly follow the course of social expectation. Marriage is the next step, it just has to be; the promise of a blissful future and the Colonial dream of security and ownership.

Still, it works as often as not, I guess. Funny how everyone around us holds firm and more invested in maintaining the illusion of our marriage than we are. Oh, how they will grieve, and preach, and judge, the family, the friendships, the church, and all the outsiders. Each from their personal fears shocked and morally affronted. How many times will I hear the placating tone, "Have you considered the children?"

"Uh, gee, no. Now that you mention it, the impact on my own children never really crossed my mind. Thank God you were there to consider them."

I returned home from the beach house with Josephine, a stranger. Sure, it was all familiar: the bicycles in the front drive, the basketball net torn from over use, the mini-van, the reusable grocery sacks neatly folded in the entry. This is becoming impossible. I've only been gone for three days and I can barely sustain the "happy to be home" expression. My wife steps away from a boiling pot to hug me. I ask, "Where are the boys?"

"At a sleep-over," Sarah winks. "How was the fishing?"

I don't think I can do this anymore, juggle two lives, conceal my passion, and pretend to be happy here. Tonight I will sit across from my wife, listen attentively, and smile appropriately. Later, in the comfort of darkness, where she's most comfortable, I will raise her flannel nightie and like a crook and a shyster infiltrate her coveted space. Then I will roll over to leave her robbed and defiled.

I dream of her. It is the dream born of an earlier conversation. As I walked with Josephine along the beach, she asked an interesting question. "Why do you think so many people are addicted to pornography?"

My answer was, "Too obvious—because our obsession with the material only leads to emptiness. Do you really imagine a bigger house, a home theater system with flat-screen plasma TV, two luxury cars in the garage, private schools, and a wine cellar can fill us or further insulate us from pain and unconsciousness? Really?"

In my dream I am bent over a naked woman. A pimp stands in the corner watching with a sick satisfying smirk. It is my smirk and I realize I am the pimp until I look down at the woman looking off in the distance, unaffected by the thrashing man and smirking pimp, and I realize she is me, too.

CHAPTER ELEVEN

I do not know if this affair will ever end. Anonymity is seductive. We have created an imaginary world for ourselves, part illusion, and part reality.

It is Tuesday again in a downtown hotel room. Beneath his heavy embrace Thomas stares into my eyes and tells me to ask for what I want. I lean in and whisper my wish for his tongue to run over my clit with his fingers inside of me until I fill his mouth and my juices run down his chin. Yes, I am one of those rare "squirters." Only it is not really a squirt and I hate that word. It is really more like a flood. It is the kind of event to which you might bring snorkeling gear and especially goggles. He drinks me up and smiles, my stream glistening off his chin.

Not being able to wait a whole week until the next Tuesday, we meet again on Thursday. He asks to take me to lunch...again. We have been spending more and more time together. I am accepting fewer contracts and Thomas is seeing fewer clients.

On this day, he drives me to the outskirts of town. We eat at this restaurant with the word "grill" on the neon sign, two of the letters are burned out. The waitress calls us "Hon" and tells us all the food is good and she has been there forever, which is obvious. Her being there forever, I mean.

This is how we spend our afternoons together, huddled in some restaurant off a side road, abandoned highway, or forgotten town.

We have a contest to see who can order the best food from the menu and then we barter. We giggle about life's ironies. Sometimes we talk politics or religion. I ask a lot of questions like, "How are small town women different from city girls?"

"What was his favorite childhood memory?" and "Who is more to blame for America's descent: corporate greed, religious tyranny, public apathy, or political narcissism?"

Of course sometimes we just make things up. Today we are discussing what we would like to look like if we did not look like ourselves. Thomas describes his new self and I laugh because in the new version of himself he still looks like a pirate, only with long hair. I explain I am not attracted to men with long hair. "This time you will have to sail your pirate ship without me."

He says, "My ship will not sail without my gypsy queen."

"Gypsy Queen" is what he calls me. He vows to capture me and hold me hostage if I will not go willingly.

I lean back in the booth, the regular lunch customers long gone, and ask, "Now tell me, Captain, what might capture look like?"

He stares at me with those piercing blue eyes and describes the scene, storming into my house, throwing me over his shoulder, and carrying me to his ship.

"Once in the ship's quarters I would rip off your clothes and chain you naked in the brig. In the evening, with the ship safely at sea, I would unlock the iron clasp around your neck and carry you to the safety of my cabin."

"There with your wrists still in shackles, I bathe you. Pouring heated water over your hair and shoulders. I would pat dry your back and breasts, and gently comb out your tangled locks. Then I would carefully dress you and feed you fresh fruit, aged cheeses, and decadent chocolate sweets. With the waves rhythmically beating against the ship, I would untie your laced nightgown and kiss you tenderly. Whether you yield to me or not, I will take you until we are both breathless and exhausted."

Pulling me in closer, he continues. "We'll sleep through the night content in each other's arms. In the morning you will again be stripped of your clothes and chained to a mahogany column in my captain's quarters."

He assures me I would not want to run naked on the ship deck with hungry scoundrel deck hands. The idea is actually more appealing than I'm willing to admit.

"When we land in ports, my gypsy queen will be dressed in women's finery and paraded through the town, showered with gifts of jewels, rare delicacies, and the most extraordinary silks and linens."

Then he leans in and whispers, "I give you my word, on the day you promise to stay beside me, I will loosen the chains forever."

I am too feral, secretly I know I would never succumb to such a promise. Not because I will not stay beside him. At this point, I have come to love the iron clasps, real or imagined.

As we leave the restaurant he grabs a handful of mints. He looks at me and with his eyes asks me if I want one.

I nod yes.

He then drops the peppermint into my mouth. I breathe in the minty freshness, the coolness curls around my tongue. Or is it hot?

Back in bed, with my naked thighs straddling my lover of the sea, I lean into his ear and ask, "What would the captain do to me if while we were in town, I would attempt an escape?

He stares me directly in the eyes and says, "I would rip off your fancy dress and carry you kicking and screaming back to my ship with the entire town watching."

I lean over him and whisper, "Hold tight to my chains, Captain."

Then I squeeze from inside, his breath grows heavy, his eyes close. Oh, a pirate's life for me!

THE BEAUTY OF FANTASY

Josephine is not a complacent soul. Her spirit requires, no, DEMANDS, vibrancy and change. She has an unyielding passion for new horizons and an insatiable appetite for the unexamined. She must, simply must, experience the razor's edge. It's anything but a quiet ride to be her chosen, rest assured—my God, how I love this about her.

Unfortunately, I know by now that love—even love that is true and unconditional—won't be enough for her. I understand it all too fucking well. For better or worse, we've been gifted this ancient pact. In this place of solidarity there comes the awareness, an inevitable acceptance of Josephine, who lives life on her own terms. While this past year has been spent together, it is clear this is not a woman who subscribes to societal expectations of monogamy. If there is no fidelity to her husband, I certainly couldn't expect it as a lover.

So what can I tell you about my gypsy's bedfellows? Enough to make me burst with laughter as Josephine describes a new suitor who has drawn her attention. She confides like a best friend, giddy and wondering. She wants to play. It's her release…underneath, I feel the briefest angst—far less for myself than for the poor son of a bitch who thinks he's won something. In the beginning, he may say all the right things. I can respect that—hardly easy to be advanced enough to get that far. What is far rarer is to be allowed a glimpse inside her veiled curtain.

Amazing, I know. But dude, seriously. This is Josephine we're talking about. Whatever you're thinking, you haven't even come close to scratching the surface. Whatever you assume or expect, however insightful you think you are… Child, please, it is a tad further from the apple than you expected to swallow. I assure you.

Ah, even in this place, I can still be the student at times, particularly on the subject of domination and submission.

It's still the truest dichotomy of her existence, a world always yielding before Josephine, offers little in the way of respite. It is simply impossible she could ever release herself fully, when for too long she has mastered control.

It was a question I had been asked first, in a moment finally trusting. Could I be the one? Could I dominate her? I knew what she was asking and why. I measured my devotion, considered my own boundaries and the limits of our relationship. I wanted to be her everything. I reached inward as far as I could, how I hated to turn her down.

During this space and time, I just couldn't. I adored Josephine too much and was uncertain about my own authority. Even as a role player I just couldn't risk intentionally hurting her. It's possible, too, I felt tentative about succumbing to my own selfish will. As a man I had practiced restraint for so long I feared the consequence of abandoning the disciplined gentleman and unleashing the troglodyte within. I feared the outcome not only for her, I feared the outcome for myself.

And so I knew, because we live the same chords, she was already seeking, already exploring. It was her time. God only knows how deep she went into the rabbit hole, what corners she pursued before selecting her match. A Dom of some experience and resonating with her on some level I don't even care to imagine. The plan was set. He scheduled her for a full weekend; making all of the travel arrangements. Her only commitment was to be his subject; willingly yield in a manner perfectly impossible in the suburban life of soccer games and legislative committees.

I guess I was supposed to react as betrayed or hurt, even devastated. I waited, it never came. I just wanted to support her and I believe even Josephine was taken a bit off guard by my response. Loyalty is my only reply.

Instead, we discussed the trip at length. In this place of acceptance, we both began to understand the depth of our love and connection beside each other. Whatever concerns I expressed were not for me. No explanation necessary. It was not for me to question her path—only to stand beside and defend wherever her course may lead. My only absolute demand when she left was for her safe return.

When I came to her on the Monday afterward, it was quiet, really quiet. Ascending the stairs on my toes, without realizing why until I saw her resting in her bath, pure and fragile as ever I'd witnessed. She was spent. Exhausted and so clearly at peace. However I hated to admit it, she was right to go.

The steam and perfumed soaps permeated the air. I folded a towel and sat down next to the bath without words, waiting in silence. She said nothing, only lifted her gaze as if searching—as if waiting to be judged.

Ah, my love. You think so? Judged? All I feel is appreciation for you and whatever serenity you have found. All I know is you are home now…safe. I kneel beside her timid, waiting spirit and touch the still water with grateful fingers. Without thinking I pick up the wash cloth and bathe her slowly. She leans in, angling her back toward me. I draw the cloth against her tender thighs, gently rinse the rope marks along her wrists. Taking the shower head, I run the water over her hair. She hands me the shampoo and follows with the conditioner. When she winces I can tell her scalp is sensitive. I cringe at the thought. I remember with reverence this precious gift, Josephine. I'm not here to possess and certainly not to direct—only to love. To wrap her in a towel and pull her in, kiss her forehead, and be the haven she needs.

I whisper, "You're safe. I love you. It's okay."

I kneel then, caressing her naked form with scented oil and closing my eyes, silently bearing fingerprints on her bruised thighs. Until I feel her curl into my arms, like a child. I carry her into the bedroom and lay her on the rug. I cover her with a blanket and listen to her breathing. An hour passes and then two, Jewel's Goodbye Alice in Wonderland is playing on the stereo, at last she pulls me into her.

"Gently," she quietly entreats.

And then I remember. I, too, have come home.

CHAPTER TWELVE

I am sitting at a stop light running through the scene from the day before: Vince came storming in, cell phone history in hand, with Thomas's number occupying 85% of the page. I reassured him. "Vince, this will not last."

"Look at how often you two are talking," he shouts, throwing the print out in my lap. Josephine, you are out of control! I bet his wife still doesn't know?"

"No," I answer picking up the papers without looking at their contents.

Regaining his composure he glares. "This is not going to end well. Do you know what you are doing?"

It is the right question to ask. The correct answer is, "I have no idea." When it comes to relationships, does anyone, really? Instead I offer the answer which will bring him the most comfort. "Honey, I know this has gotten out of hand. We are going to put some distance between us and take a break. You and the kids are the most important part of my life. I will not compromise our family."

"Really, Jo? I'm afraid we're way beyond that."

Walking away with his back to me he says, "This was never part of our agreement either!" Sometimes I wish Vince would demand the end to this affair. You have to know Vince to know why he would never make any demands. See, first he would have to take off his white gloves and get his hands dirty with emotional intimacy. That zone is off limits. Second, he likes to wear the martyr banner like a badge of honor. There is this story he lives and it goes something like this, "If you aren't suffering, you aren't living." Lastly, if he has to feel something, his default is guilt. If he actually put his foot down and demanded I stop taking lovers, he would feel guilty I was not getting what I wanted. So he walks around with white gloves, a pretty martyr banner, and the satisfaction of never saying no while I go fuck myself silly. It works...usually.

We are struggling in our marriage. It has been two months and he still has not forgiven my weekend adventure into the unfamiliar world of BDSM. He has learned to tolerate the occasional afternoon with Thomas, he is working and unaffected. My absence over the course of a weekend and the knowledge I had intentionally placed myself in danger was too great of a risk. I tried to explain it was only my way of better examining my ego defenses and summoning the distant experience of vulnerability I keep avoiding. A stranger governing me was too great of a request for Vince to accept. I went anyway, even after he refused to give his consent and for the first time, our agreement had been violated.

I had to ask myself, was I pushing Vince away? Or, was I doing battle with my own fears and insecurities in the only realm where I would allow myself to completely surrender?

When I think of Vince and our marriage, I imagine an ancient castle. It is made of precisely cut stones. It is surrounded by a deep cool moat. There is a drawbridge. We can come and go freely yet the castle itself is safeguarded. I wake each morning in the kingdom and tend to him and our beloved children. On occasion I walk barefoot through the green forests and meadows outside. Always I return to him, this is where I reside. For the gypsy spirit I am, the promise to stay, is something.

RESTORING THE WALLS

I see it in her eyes...I know what is coming...
Josephine has been distant. I haven't seen her in a couple of weeks and the time ticked by so slowly I thought I would go mad. She meets me at my office. She is unchanged, confident and unshakable. The ultimate enigma intelligent, intuitive, kind, powerful, dedicated to people, especially the most fragile among us and absolutely rebellious.

That's her and it always will be.

If you want to live in her world, above the ridiculous fray, never sweat, never sink to quiet moodiness, and never succumb to fear. Weakness repels her, especially in a man. To actually NEED her as in processing some deep fear or insecurity —it's really much better to simply shut it down and piss her off for being suddenly unavailable. Anger is temporary, her resistance to the timid male is absolute. Those circumstances take a bit more time and effort to rectify.

When she turns away, it's with full commitment. Trust me. She is drawn to a truly strong, endlessly secure, assertive male who knows his own power. Hard-to-get makes her wet. She plays outside the mundane and boys aren't allowed.

She stands in my doorway wearing jeans and red cowboy boots. "Hi, stranger! Were you lost without me? Then she closes the door behind her and I roll back my chair so she can slide onto my lap and into my arms.

I hold her, this powerhouse of soulful wisdom, where underneath still lives a frightened little girl who wants to lean into strength not her own, to rest in arms solid and certain.

I have my own needs and vulnerabilities. Every time she withdraws, accepts another lover, or disappears into the sunset, I think my heart will cease to beat. I feel the cold coagulate in my veins and I wait for the last breath to come. It comes followed by another breath and another after that. Eventually I pick myself up carried by the hopeful anticipation of Josephine's return.

I can feel her defenses raised. I wanted to spend the day caressing her in bed. She said she had "a million things to catch up on." We sit having lunch instead. I heard the retreat in her voice when she called. Now I watch it in her body language. She picks a restaurant near my office, something we never do. She is sitting across from me instead of next to me. She tells me about her work. Josephine loves her job. I love being her escape. Today she is all business. I kiss her and say goodbye closing the car door. She smiles back at me through the closed window. The words are left unspoken. I feel the dismissal coming...

Throughout these years there has only been one person with whom I have confided. Jim lives in Pennsylvania, a distance seemingly safe enough. We also met through our wives and spent plenty of time together when our children were new to the world and families were budding. Our kids were the same age and it was an enormous loss when about five years ago they moved for a job opportunity and to be closer to his wife's family. Strangely our friendship began after the move. He confided in me only after his affair with a young, married co-worker had resulted in the end of his marriage. Initially his wife Elizabeth tried to save the marriage, but when it was clear Jim wasn't going to end the affair, she filed for divorce. They were a beautiful family, everyone who knew them grieved the loss. I knew Jim and Elizabeth offered foreshadowing for the potential of my own life, the essence of the types of disaster we should all try to avoid.

Jim and I would share at length the complexities of being men, husbands and fathers, and also wanting to be loved and nurtured, to feel the moments of comfort and pleasure beyond obligation and responsibility. Is it so wrong to be reckless in the arena of love and intimacy and why can this option feel so elusive in the context of marriage?

In the end, Jim didn't get the girl. She remained with her husband while Elizabeth met another man and moved him into their family home. Eventually he claimed her as his bride. I heard she wore a white dress nearly identical to the first wedding dress. Jim sees his two kids on the weekends now. It's the conclusion I fear in my own story. I don't want to be relegated to weekends only with my boys or left alone without Josephine.

I pour myself a glass of Scotch, light a cigar, and begin dialing Jim.

CHAPTER THIRTEEN

Gradually I had begun the process of untethering myself from Thomas. Since the trip away and the confrontation with Vince, I was unwinding the tendrils binding the two of us. Intuitively, I knew the cost of our love had grown too great and it was compromising my family. Despite my romantic adventures, family has always been paramount to me.

I had not quite jumped Thomas's ship, I was dangling behind clinging to a life preserver while looking for dry land. It was gradual, mostly because I was not sure I would be able to let go. I was, however, attempting to leave the relationship and I know Thomas felt the separation.

Just as I was beginning to make progress I received a phone call.

"Can you meet me? It's important."

I didn't want to, although I could hear something in his voice... desperation.

"What is it?" I asked.

He paused, knowing my reservation. "I can't talk about it over the phone. I really need to see you."

We made plans to see each other the next day at the lake not far from our homes.

I prepared my grandmother's recipe of Chicken Cacciatore and paid close attention to Vince as he talked about the events at work. The kids squabbled over a missing shirt and claims were made against the "borrower" who refused to acknowledge any blame.

Laundry piles were sorted until the missing shirt was found crumpled in the back of a closet and order was restored. It was a standard evening of dirty dishes, homework, and easy conversations. As the sun was setting behind the mountain peaks, my daughters and I walked the dogs through the neighborhood of leafless trees and lighted windows. Garage doors opened and closed signaling the workday's end.

This was simple. Expectations were met, security attained. It was predictable. It was our lives, the life I valued most.

TROUBLED WATERS

From a distant fog I watch every hushed and concerned tone; each saddened, quiet turn aside of a nurse or lab technician trying to sound desperately hopeful while backing slowly out of the room. Specialist physicians scan the reports and fall silent. Too often those upturned eyes empathically peering over half glasses, searching to find the right words. The message all too clear—the rules no longer hold any sway.

The discovery: this is the end of charted waters. I can pull sail and drift with the tide or rudder hard into the wind, the forever uncertain future. I glimpse the end; it is a banquet table set with every measure of extravagance. A feast of plenty with all we desire and value most so carefully presented on the finest mirror polished platters and wares. Goblets brimming with all the possibilities gifted in each simple day. The flavors are beyond imagination and there is a timeless beauty in every perspective.

To the ear, life is a symphony: the chattering of a small bird, rain on the pavement, and the laughter of children. To the heart, whatever its capacity, there is no space except to love purely. And the whole of the banquet, all of it, lit by the flames of freedom—for there are no longer dreams to be wasted on material endeavors or social obligations.

I find a new resolve—while I am alive on this planet, breathing in this body, I plan to tap every last vestige of life.

CHAPTER FOURTEEN

Since we first began, we have slowly and methodically separated any former ties between our families. I have not seen his wife Sarah since the Fall Festival over a year ago. It was a risk and a discomfort both Thomas and I never want to re-live again. We both knew we were in the wrong and until now were not willing to give it up. We simply added a romantic life to our home and work lives. For a while it became routine. Thomas had an afternoon block on my weekly schedule. If an opportunity came up for both of us to connect, we took that, too.

Thomas was becoming integrated into my life. His emotional support was feeling like something of a necessity. Vince, expecting this tryst would have already met its fate and I would have long since moved onto another, was beginning to express anxiety and resentment.

I knew something had to change…we all did.

On this Tuesday morning, as I pull into the gravel parking lot, Thomas is already waiting. I feel this hollow in the pit of my stomach. His skin is white and he wears a look I have never seen before.

Instead of getting in the car, he opens my car door and asks, "Walk?"

"Sure," I answer grabbing a coat from the back.

"I have to tell you something."

I slip my hand inside his large calloused palm.

As we walk the frozen ground he shares the story. A couple of weeks ago he began having chest pains. His primary care doctor made the referral to the cardiologist. It was Dr. Kerry who had diagnosed Hypertrophic cardiomyopathy and Familial combined hyperlipidemia.

I look at him confused. I knew both his father and grandfather had died before the age of fifty from heart attacks, the genetic ramifications did not sink in until this moment.

"What's the prognosis?" I ask concerned.

"It's not good. My body produces a cholesterol which aggressively builds plaque and with the combined weak heart muscle there's not adequate blood being supplied consistently."

I stop on the trail where there is a place to rest. While he sits, I stand and face him. His arms reach around my sides and pull me in. "Isn't there a medication or a surgical procedure for treatment?"

"These are both pretty rare conditions. The doctors are especially concerned because I already take good care of diet and exercise. This is my genetic inheritance. They prescribed several medications and now I will forever be monitored very closely."

"Are you a candidate for a heart transplant?"

"Even if I was, I'm not going that route. It may be a worn out heart, but it's mine."

I look deep into his blue eyes to find the reassurance this would also pass, that life and love are not indeed temporary states. A world without Thomas had been the goal I was working towards. And yet, this new reality of a future where my love would be gone forever, registers as inconceivable.

On the drive home, I call my friend Amanda and talk it through. I offer the full story of trying to leave and the devastating realization of not wanting to lose him. She's pragmatic and neutral, knowing both Vince and Thomas.

"You know honey, I was totally against this in the beginning. I was concerned for everyone too much would be sacrificed. I've watched you over these past couple of years and you seem happy, really happy. Vince will stay by your side no matter what. He is completely dedicated to you. Having lost my mother to a heart-attack, I would do just about anything for some more time together. If you

are certain you can sustain both your marriage and this love affair, well, this may be all you have together."

I consider the possibility Thomas's condition is self-induced, the manifestation of a broken heart. The subconscious and conscious are quite capable of manipulating both our physical and psychological realities. I also practice a faith where everything and everyone is an expression of the divine unfolding, including the meddling with our egos. So after further investigation into his condition, I accepted the idea, even if the heart disease was Thomas' manifestation, as part of some divine intervention.

I recognized the moment as my last opportunity to be free of his inexorable binds. I did not escape.

NO ACCIDENT

Eventually Josephine and I settled into our old routine. Our days were still Tuesdays and I waited every day for it to be Tuesday again.

In early spring, we found a chance to get away. The calendar shifted and the family was unexpectedly booked out of town. It was spring break and during the work week, a time when I couldn't join them.

I would give anything…anything for a night with Josephine, even one single night without the din and entanglements of life. It didn't matter how much time we had together, there was the awareness I could never get enough of her.

So we drove away, her hand caressing mine as I touched her thigh, energy and anticipation. A moment of concurrence as our fingers intertwined and held.

The whole experience pulled me into a forgotten time—the incredible, fantastical realm of first love. Like the naive innocence characterizing youthful ideals, a time when anything is possible and the future…limitless. I felt myself falling forever in love, having the wisdom of experience to fully appreciate the rarity and magnitude of this gift.

And whatever I knew or believed before those days and nights together was forever altered then. It was nothing like before. I felt no hesitation, no question between us. Every barrier dissolved. Undressing her, I knew she was with me. Touching her breast, I felt only release. Opening her hips, I knew her last resistance had finally yielded. Our connection wasn't going to fade, no matter the course or the costs. Our time had come.

CHAPTER FIFTEEN

I have this image of me as a child running on the outer banks of a lake. I may have seen it in a picture once. The thing is, I have never felt myself not running, whether running from something, toward something, or for the simple joy of feeling the wind in my hair and the light ahead. It is not a malady or a psychological defect. For me it has been a state of being. I have not recognized this state as a lack or deficiency, until now.

Whether it is the quiet moments I spend in his arms or the strong calm of his soul, Thomas has taught me not to struggle, he has shown me the stillness lies just beneath the noise. I love his sanctuary. Thomas brings my face to his chest and he runs his hands through my hair again. He pulls me into his lap, wraps his arms around me, and instantly I am at peace.

In my dream I am a child again. This time I timidly approach a vast lake. Gradually I walk out and touch the tip of my toes to the water. Eventually I wade in past my knees. The chill chases me to the shore again. I hear his voice, "Take my hand." All this time, I have been like a fearful child.

I am done resisting...everything, including Thomas. I want to submerge myself in the cool of this water, to feel my entire body float in the depths of this love. In this moment I do not want to feel the wind at my face. I want the stillness, the darkness, and him.

I am finished running.

Thomas and I steal away for a couple of days. My choices are not defensible. We choose an old Inn in a faraway corner. When we arrive, the writing on the chalkboard greets us, "Welcome, Mr. and Mrs. Wright."

We grin and our hands reach out to find each other again. Thomas booked the honeymoon suite. In my head it is spelled "honey moon sweet." The bed is brass and covered with antique white linens. The corner boasts an old-fashioned oval mirror.

While Thomas sits on the edge of the bed, I watch in the mirror as he frees each of my buttons, opening my white cotton top, exposing my chest. He gently unzips my shorts, slips off my leather sandals, and drops my shorts to the floor. He does not rush. I have worn panties just to watch him slide them over my thighs and past the tips of my toes. I stand naked and exposed as he looks me over, runs his fingers along my curves, touching my softness. I simply wait. When he is ready he takes me in his arms and we make love.

At dinnertime we drive to an ancient log cabin recently converted into a restaurant. It is surprisingly crowded for this small mountain town. We sit at the bar and wait. Despite, his doctor's orders, Thomas drinks his wheat beer and I sip a glass of Merlot. For dinner the hostess sits us right in front of the musician who serenades us with acoustical renditions of songs of love and revolution from the '60s and '70s. Sometimes my life feels like a dream.

After dinner we walk to a hole-in–the-wall bar. A live band plays on stage and the crowd is an interesting mixture of overpaid yuppies and over-lived renegades. I honestly do not know to which group we belong. By the drinks in our hands, it would have to be the former. When I grow up, though, I want to be a biker chick, or at least wear a pair of those leather chaps.

When Thomas returns from the bar, I have carved our names into the table which is the décor for this particular establishment. If you sit at our same table you will see the heart encircling the names, "Thomas + Josephine." When I come back from the restroom, Thomas has added the word "forever." I feel giddy, like a silly teenager.

As the band begins a new set, I stand up to dance. My body moves with the rhythm and I leave the world of thought and enter the world of movement. Thomas leans back in his chair, tilts the neck of his Fat Tire beer, and watches every swirl of my hips. When the band finishes playing the set, he places his money on the table and reaches for my hand, silently leading me out of the bar.

Back at the Inn we wrap our bodies in terrycloth robes and walk to the outside Jacuzzi. We wrap ourselves in this bubble of privilege and stare up at the sky amassed with stars. Despite a cool breeze, the water is hot. Thomas sits in a seat along the edge of the tub. I straddle him and the water rises with my hips.

I can feel him deep inside me, penetrating beyond my flesh. I stare into his deep blue eyes and want to be separate no more. So comes the moment. I ask, "Will you live with me in the cottage by the sea?"

He smiles back at me. "Shall we make a secret promise?"

Nodding, I can see he wants it more than anything he has ever wanted before.

With the water splashing against the sides and Thomas filling the whole of me, I promise to marry him on a hill under an ancient tree. In my head it is so clear, a warm spring afternoon, encircled by meadows of wild flowers and the birds and the blossoms as our witness.

I whisper in his ear, "I will wear a simple white dress, transparent in the sunlight with purple delicate lavender flowers crowning my head."

He says, "Can you hear the words? Do you take this man…?"

And looking back into Thomas's eyes, I answer,

"I do."

"I do."

"I do."

Forever is not long enough.

HOPE AND A PROMISE

Her ring on my cell phone, "Wild thing…you make my heart sing." Why can't I hear her ring without smiling?

"Hello, gorgeous."

"How late?"

"Are you alone?"

"I'm on my way."

Only blocks from her house and I realize…I'm still smiling.

CHAPTER SIXTEEN

Proclamations are a funny thing. As soon as you make a proclamation you are given the opportunity to test its merits. My menstrual cycle is three days late. Not only am I running again, I am at a full sprint. Thomas came inside of me. My period had only ended a couple of days before so technically I should be okay. Yet here I am, always with periods 28 days apart, only this time I am 72 hours late.

All I can think of is, "Oh my God, what have I done?" I do not want to have an abortion. I do not want my husband to raise someone else's child. I do not want to leave my children and my family to make a new one, even if it is with Thomas.

I told Thomas my period was late. I think he is trying to hide his happiness. He is saying all of the right things, while the sense of panic here is most certainly not shared.

Thomas and I really respect each other as parents. He is an extraordinary father, not just because he is the basketball coach, the Boy Scout leader, and the prehistoric dragon, which he is. He is a great father because he knows his children. He hears them, he understands them, and he shares himself, too. I do not know where he finds the time for it all, work, family, me. I do know his children are his top priority.

I feel the same way. I may compromise in other areas, I will not compromise my children, not intentionally, anyway. A beautiful childhood is the thing I want most for my daughters. Not the Martha Stewart kind where the table linens match and the birthday party favors are appropriately themed. I want them to have the kind of childhood where they play freely, live carelessly, and discover themselves. I want them to crawl in their beds each night with a feeling of safety and rise each morning with a sense of possibility.

I love being a mother. In this complicated world, the role of mother and child is the only role which makes perfect sense to me. The moments when they come running in to share their day, or we sit reading books together our feet entangled, or all of the thousands of common place exchanges, they are most precious to me.

There are times when I close my eyes and I can see myself with Thomas...waking up in the beach house to the smell of coffee and his hands rubbing my rounded tummy. When I became pregnant with my second daughter, I felt like I was betraying the first. As if this sacred bond we had shared would now be broken, my womb now inhabited by someone new.

I was so careful to make sure my older daughter felt included. She helped decorate the nursery, we read books about babies and I helped her to feel important as the big sister. When her baby sister was finally born, it was the best gift she had ever been given. My two daughters have always been very close. There's nothing more important to me than being a great mother.

Still, there's absolutely no way I would be willing to have another child. My body, I can share, but my life is already spoken for. There's nothing I would allow to come between me and my children, not even another child. It's simply something I will not reconcile.

My girlfriends wonder how I can sustain two relationships. I answer cheekily, "The same way I sustain multiple friendships." Love is not limited and you do not have to ration yourself. My experience is abundance and I live in a world of soul sovereignty. I do not have to choose between my husband and Thomas, I can have them both, and I do. There are limitations, however, and I acknowledge those, too. Although people change families all the time, children are not interchangeable. Their sense of identity and belonging are very much linked to their parents and family.

Also, I do not want two marriages and two families. I want one, the one I have created. My life is no accident. I chose my husband carefully and I chose well. There has not been one day I have regretted sharing my life with him. Our decision to have children was intentional and planned. Although parents never fully understand the sacrifice, I was prepared to dedicate myself wholly to the care of our babies. Every decision I have made since their births has been with their well-being in mind. Although I have compartmentalized Thomas, our relationship has made me happier, more relaxed, and a better parent. He loves in a way I never learned. Connection is expressed through touch. Because of Thomas, I am able to give more physical affection to my children. At night I rub their backs and shower them with hugs and kisses. The question now of a possible pregnancy brings all of my favorite images into focus.

Many years ago I took a spirituality class called "A Course in Miracles." One of the exercises was to look at everything and recognize God. I remember looking at a tree and thinking, "So this is what God looks like." I'd see a mountain and say, "Good morning, God." Eventually what I learned through the exercise was this: spirit is where we see it. I began to look for the divine in all things, including the figments present in our own imagination.

I do not know what I will do if I am pregnant. I do know this, my figment of imagination is one in which my children grow up in the security of two loving parents. I am determined whatever drama or chaos I create privately will not cause havoc in their innocent lives. The world is crazy enough. We may just be beginning to reclaim some awareness in the collective conscience, teetering on the brink of insanity. I cannot spare my children from hurt, shelter them from disappointment, or guarantee their happiness. I can show up for them, honor them, care for them, and appropriately model humanity in all her divine folly.

PENANCE

I should be worried and thinking, "How am I going to tell Sarah?" Instead, I sleep soundly dreaming of naked wrinkled birds with beaks open awaiting sustenance. I take notice of the nest…down filled, hallowed, and high above the world.

Josephine has courted guilt. She wants me to join her knees to the ground in flagellation. This time I can't capitulate. I have never questioned this path, ever. It is the only place for me where truth resonates unimpeded. I do have this one final regret, that others may ultimately suffer from the love Jo and I share.

On that day you will find me on my knees. I will do my penance then, I do not atone for my sins or ask for the redemption of this soul, not in this moment.

I pick up the phone to call Jim. It's been awhile. Last time we spoke I told him about Vince coming home to my car on the street and his wife's head resting in my lap. Both his disapproval and the recognition we crossed over some imaginary line, left me stinging.

"Hey, man." I tell him what's up because he's the only place I can confide.

"Tom," he says. "I know you love her, but I don't think you're thinking this through. You know where this is headed, people are going to get hurt and it's the people you love the most."

I know he's right. I tell him, "At this point, I can't imagine being without her. Every time we're together, I'm the happiest

I've ever been. It's the time away from Josephine I find unbearable."

Jim asks, "Is it time for you to leave Sarah?"

I let the question dangle in the air. I'm thinking back to a conversation we had a year ago. At dinner one evening Sarah said, "I figured out why Jess and Michael got a divorce."

"Why?" I replied.

"Because they weren't having sex."

I simply raised my eyebrows and changed the subject because I already knew where both the conversation and our own relationship was headed.

"What would be my incentive to leave?" I ask into the phone. "Josephine has no intention of leaving Vince. He doesn't seem to mind she has frosting all over her face, so long as she's smiling. Why should she make any changes? Even if there's a child, I have no guarantee Jo would even stay with me."

"Seriously, dude. You think you're going to get another woman pregnant and your wife isn't going to find out! Trust me, man. Sarah is going to figure this out eventually, they always do."

"She seems pretty content to be left alone. At least we're not fighting about sex anymore."

"I'm asking this as a friend, how are you going to start to address this whole affair in a way that's going to allow you to like yourself?"

After we hang up, I watch the amber scotch fall over the ice cubes in my glass and imagine lying next to Josephine resting my head against her swollen womb pulsing with new life—a life that is ours.

CHAPTER SEVENTEEN

So, I am not pregnant. This story does not end in a beach house with a baby. Not on this page, anyway.

The next time we are together, Thomas asks me if I want him to get a vasectomy. I say, "I don't care," which is the truth. Then I add, "If I become pregnant, it will be the end of our magical love affair."

He will not get the vasectomy. Other men want my heart, my laughter, and my warm spaces. Thomas wants my belly, round with the promise of tomorrow. There are times when I share this dream, when I lean in and describe our child. "Big blue eyes, rosy cheeks, dark curls, eating her cherub pink toes and giggling between us."

On this occasion I do not resort to those means of "dirty talk." I am distant. Scared, mostly, that something I want is in direct contrast with the something else I want. Frustration comes easier to me than Thomas. During these times when I start to overthink the relationship and our future, Thomas grabs hold of me. He answers my questions patiently, "Yes, I want to spend every night and every day with you."

"Of course I would give anything to be with you."

Then he says, "Trust my love, our connection is stronger than time and space, and all else."

My eyes convey my doubts. He leads me to an anonymous bed and undresses me. A duffle hidden under the frame is pulled out into the light. I watch in surprise, although I have observed this scene before. He straps the loop around my ankles and secures the ropes around the feet of the bed. My wrist is buried beneath a sheet. He grabs it forcefully and gently and secures it to the headboard. I extend my other wrist to him obediently and within seconds I am bound and under his complete control. He whispers in my ear, "Are you mine?"

I answer coyly, "Today I am."

"That is not enough." He spreads my thighs and brings his tongue down on me. At first he moves slowly, gliding his fingers inside of me, tasting me. Then his tongue beats against my tender spot and at the moment before I climax, he suddenly stops. He rises up to look in my eyes and asks again, "Are you mine?"

I try to find the words, something cheeky or romantic, I am distracted. The words will not come. It is the rarest occasion when my body overrides my brain. Thomas does not wait. He only smiles. He ties on the blindfold to cover my eyes. I bring my legs together, he opens them and his tongue eventually brings me to the same glorious edge. This time I am more prepared. When he asks again, "Are you mine?" I start in on a carefully rationalized and detailed explanation.

To which Thomas responds by placing a gag in my mouth. He unties my legs turns me over face down. Out of the bag I hear the jingling of steel links, a large circle in the middle connects to four short chains with a ring on each end. I feel the cold metal ring being placed on the small of my back. He moves my wrist and ankle restraints from the bedposts and connects each limb to its accompanying chain. I am hog tied on my stomach. Still gagged and blindfolded he buries his tongue and fingers from a different angle. I am dripping wet with craving. My muscles quiver beyond my control. My moans are muffled and yet understood, I cannot bear to be denied any longer. He holds out. Kissing me tenderly, running his fingers through my hair.

Finally, he removes the blindfold, "Are you mine?"

I nod with my eyes, "Yes."

He unties the gag.

"Are you mine forever?" he asks.

"Yes," I reply.

My body, I give to him.

As he slips his fingers inside of me, I momentarily leave the earthly realm for the secret place of bliss where there is no sound and no form and total beauty. As the sensation nears, I return to my home of skin, bone, and sinew. The muscles inside of me involuntarily tighten as the muscles outside breathe the exquisite sigh of release. Thomas catches the last of it in his mouth and drinks me up. Only he is not done. When he comes inside of me this time, it is the forbidden place he fills. Thomas has a funny way of making amends.

SHE IS MINE?

"What do you want?" Not a question to be taken lightly. Not from Josephine. Her intent is to know "What is the deepest, most elusive, or even taboo fantasy I can indulge for you?"

The immediate whispers, "It's enough, it's a million times more than enough." There's nothing more I need or want to ask from this ray of pure light. It is enough to experience her surrender against my chest or to reach for her mouth and feel her desire. Yet, this is one of those times requiring the abandonment of subtlety.

In time, Josephine has taught me the art of sexual play. Despite the years of marriage without intimacy, my dreams quietly locked away in a distant lifetime, I too felt the budding desire to rid myself of the constant menial pursuit of approval and just submit to the deep, raw sexuality and the intemperate satisfaction of my own imagination.

In the passing of these years, slowly, very slowly, I become acquainted with my own strength. Beside her, I recall my ancient lineage of nobility and masculinity. Any lingering reservations or boyish insecurities are mostly squelched.

The pact held. The pirate hold on the gypsy queen was unleashed like a high wind to the sail. Finally. No turning back and no hope for redemption. Passion and rage, forced thighs wide, Josephine defies and resists as only the powerful can. Too late. Way too late. And I knew—for once, she was not going to win. For once, she would yield or pay dearly. I was calm. I knew, “I’m going to have you, no matter how you fight or run. Scream and rip, tear and kick, I’m going to have you.”

She was mine—finally. At last. Bound, naked, and immobilized is the only path to her vulnerability. There is no greater ecstasy than a powerful woman losing herself. Feeling her claw for release and finding it in you. I have discovered what I desire most is her innocence, far beyond the soft cotton pink panties hiding young secrets, I want to command not only her body, I want to command her heart.

Possession is a dire and devilish pursuit.

CHAPTER EIGHTEEN

Thomas and I have settled into a familiar pattern. We talk every day and once, sometimes twice, a week we embark on a new adventure. He takes me to art galleries and farmers markets. Afternoons may be spent in the park or at a café. Last week I brought a picnic dinner to his office after everyone had gone home. We sat on a blanket on the floor drinking Chardonnay and telling secrets. My favorite escapades are when we get away for the day and visit some historic town. We find a quaint little restaurant and then meander through the shops holding hands like everyday couples.

For a while we may permit ourselves to be carried away in this magical love story. There are moments when we become too attached, too routine, and everything begins to get muddled. We over-identify or want more than the other can give. He wants me to run away with him and I want him to live forever.

In all of the years we have been together, Thomas has not asked me about my husband. Once I asked him if he ever got jealous. He explained there were times when he wanted to talk to me and knew he could not call, the anger and jealousy would surface and he would have to busy himself with some distraction.

Although our affair is most certainly a betrayal, love in every form is sacred. It transcends the expectations of fidelity and beliefs of morality. The honesty, acceptance, and connection Thomas and I share are deeper than any social constructs. When you experience something like this, you do not want to question, deny, or excuse it away. You want to roll around in it and immerse yourself in the filth of it and call it something beautiful.

Sometimes I consider the possibility of running off together. On the occasional Tuesday when we are headed toward a blue sky, I wish he would just keep driving. Other times he threatens to steal me away. Mostly it is a fantasy, an indulgence we entertain on rare occasions. There are times when we are together and imagine various getaways: an abandoned cabin in the woods, some far-off cave in a rolling valley, the attic of the governor's mansion, a sailboat in Fiji. My favorite image of our hide-away is a four-poster bed in a treehouse built above a river.

It is possible some day when we return home, it will be to each other. The outcome of this love story does not really matter. Thomas and I have learned to live in the moment. We can appreciate today without the promise of a tomorrow.

I love my husband, too. I wonder if Thomas and I were to move in together if I would not be running off to spend my evenings with Vince. The rhythm of his breathing and his body next to mine is familiar to me. My husband gives me flexibility and complete acceptance. He struggles at times and so do I, we have also arrived at the height of commitment. We have learned to love and simultaneously let go. I am grateful for Vince, his strong sense of self and for a union without conditions. We have traded the excitement of uncertainty for the comfort of marriage, and for the most part, I am content here, too.

It seems when you reach a place of acceptance, circumstances are irrelevant. The challenge is not in finding the "right person," the challenge is in "being" the right person—You! In fact, learning to be ourselves openly and completely is the only task we have a real chance of getting right in this lifetime.

Partners, children, careers, body weight, it is all secondary to the real questions we must answer. "Who am I?" This is the question I plan to spend each day answering. I may take Sundays off since it is the day of the Sabbath, which apparently used to be Saturdays. For historical accuracy I really should take both days off. Saturdays, Sundays, and Tuesdays…those are my days off.

Have you seen the bumper sticker that reads, "'God is dead'—

Nietzsche." Underneath are the words, "'Nietzsche is dead'—God." Several years ago at a conference in California, I met a brilliant writer and professor. We stayed up until dawn drinking cheap wine, a conference gift, and discussing philosophy, religion, politics, and education. When it came to the subject of dying and the afterlife, he having a Judeo affiliation and me with my Catholic beginning and Buddhist orientation made it clear there would be no agreement. Late into the night he sat up straight and declared, "I allege a person's perspective regarding the afterlife governs their value system."

I was thinking, "Regardless of your values or your religious associations, the outcome is still the same. Believe whatever you want about the afterlife, it may change what you value or how you live. When it comes to dying however, differences in faith, have no bearing."

It was late and not wanting to further debate, I said, "That is a likely assumption. For the most part, I have given up on the answers, instead I am learning to master the questions." This pretty much sums it up for us modern-day existentialists.

IDEALISTS

What could I desire more than any treasure?
What wish most sublime?
If I could ask the universe to grant one final gift,
One last precious moment of clarity and truth,
It would be this:

To be by your side…
And feel your hand absently stroking my back,
As you ponder trinkets in some quaint shop.
Or touching my leg when you tell a story.

To hear your laughter,
At some ridiculous common wit,
Only the two of us get.

To see your radiance fill a room, and stand aside
To watch them turn uncertainly, adjust-
ing to such fullness and light -
And you taking no notice.

To feel you lean just slightly against me,
So that I must put my arm around you
As we walk together.

To watch your face, your movements beyond awareness

As you work at some task. And turning to see me,
You smile and reach out your hand.

To feel your worn and weary brow
Find comfort on my shoulder, and saying nothing,
Your body releases itself and melts without care.

To watch you dance, your hands turning in the air,
Your whole being absorbing the enchanted moment,
And you play and know nothing else.

To feel you push back against me, as we lay,
Seeking my enfolding warmth and safety.
And listen to your breath, and touch your skin,
And feel you fall asleep at last.

These are my treasures. To me, wealth beyond compare.
All I could wish and more, has already been granted.

Thomas Wright

CHAPTER NINETEEN

Driving home from a late lunch, I got cold. Thomas slipped off his coat at a red light and handed it to me. When the sun was in my eyes and I complained of my broken sunglasses, he offered his to me. I began a round of sneezing and with one hand still on the wheel he reached behind my seat and had a tissue waiting for me before I finished the final sneeze. Sometimes I wonder what the fuck I am waiting for.

It has been a year since Thomas was diagnosed. We're nearly four years into this love affair and five if you count the year of emails and phone calls. We both have gained a valuable lesson in living. The possibility of losing something, life and love, has taught us a greater appreciation for the simple things. We play and explore together, living outside the world of lists, obligations, time lines, and responsibility. The moments are brief, a few hours at most, still, the memory of our time lingers until the next time we are together.

The line between fantasy and reality is a fine one. Even though I already know the answer, I find myself wanting to test the magic of our illicit romance against the constraints of paying a mortgage, doing household chores, and child rearing. The first years, of course would be wonderful; but could we sustain the same enthusiasm this morning's lovemaking had generated? Would we exult equally in the daily orgasm as we had in our earlier climax, delayed by the weeks of holiday interruptions and family commitments

Possibly. What I marvel at most is the way Thomas has mastered my dual nature. Like how he knows when to touch me tenderly and when it is his fist wrapped around my hair I crave most. How he skillfully brings his mouth to my nipples for an explosive finale. Or the way he coaxes me with threats or praise, hypnotizing me until I am writhing beneath him begging for him to ease the ache buried inside of me.

I marvel, too, how he knows when to reach for my hand instead of my zipper. How he gently brings his mouth to my forehead when I am on the edge of tears. Or the way he listens intently and patiently until I am emptied of whatever worry or sadness. I have never felt more seen, more understood, or more appreciated.

When it is all over and we have made love for the third time and he grabs his jacket to leave and return home to his wife, anger and resentment rise to the surface. In my mind I vow never to leave Vince. I doze off to sleep determined to hold onto the realities of marriage and family.

Then he calls just when I am waking, before I even remember he has left my side. Of course I refuse to pick up the phone. His message is brief, "Good morning, beautiful. I don't remember your appointment time. You're probably in the shower. As you go about your day just know I adore you."

I answer by melting and returning to my longing for him.

FATHERHOOD

It's late, calm, and very quiet here in this mountain cabin. I was up early, too, watching some does feed on their way to the river, listening to a distant wild turkey and then a host of chattering jays fighting over breakfast while sipping coffee and reading. In between, the boys howl, and climb, and throw, and chase. They discover interesting rocks to display on the picnic table, sword-sized sticks for battle, and the odd new insect to capture, inspect, and finally release.

It rained hard tonight—nothing a battered old cowboy hat and a flannel shirt couldn't handle...and certainly not enough to squelch the youngsters' obligatory marshmallow roast. They were soaked to the skin, there are priorities, after all. They fall asleep late...don't want to miss anything in these hills.

Then I remember. This is where I belong. It's a feeling as old as I can recall. I'm never more "myself" than I am in the solitude of the mountains. I've been coming here since I was their age and hiked and explored these old deer trails before and throughout the trials of adolescence. I learned to fly fish on these streams and I remember the old-timers who built these cabins and took some pride in teaching me their lore.

They're all gone now, still, I watch my boys and sense a sort of timeless vibrancy in and among these pines and valleys. I wish I could replay it for them, introduce them to those elders and recall for them the magic I learned here. I watch them run and realize it's becoming a part of them, and they don't realize it. I make passing observations about the history here, the nuances of the river, the fragile life around them, and the importance of simplicity and conservation. The wonder and understanding in their eyes says it all.

Of course, it is always the children. If you ever feel lost or forget the meaning, separate from the pure grace of this one lifetime—the absolute wonderment of it all, then look at life through the eyes of a child.

Funny how most of the answers I sought didn't come from the books I read or the classes I attended, or the scholars I listened to with rapt attention. They most often came in the simple moments of touching, or quietly holding, or listening to the revelations of these precious gifts—our children.

I sometimes wonder if they'll ever realize what an honor it is and has been to me, to have been granted these moments.

Probably not…

The little ingrates.

And I think too of Josephine, and this path we have chosen. I wish she could be here to share this part of me and see me as my favorite self.

Our paths run parallel. In my heart, I ache because I know this way has the potential for such possibility and destruction. It's in these moments I know the importance of our experiences together. I wish I could share them all—I wish we could walk every step together.

I see the beauty in both worlds. Yet there are occasions I struggle with how to live in both places. In my darkest moments of confusion I pull a piece of paper from my wallet. This is what guides me:

> "We try to be logical, but there's no way around it—we end up believing in whatever we think is beautiful, whether we can prove it makes sense or not. Everyone needs something wonderful in their life that they can't explain, and that they might not explain even if they could."
>
> —John Gierach

CHAPTER TWENTY

When I sat next to Vince tonight, he very gently nudged me away. The greatest insult of all came when he quit eating my dinners. I first noticed when he returned a plate full of homemade rigatoni and meatballs. I spent a whole week preparing every one of his favorite dishes, paella, braised short ribs, scallops in garlic sauce, chicken Piccata and stuffed bell peppers. He had a new excuse for not eating any of them. Rejection appears in the subtleties, a glance in the opposite direction, an interrupted sentence, a physical withdrawal. The literal world speaks clearly to me. Withholding love is only slightly different from betraying love.

I hate generalizations. People who generalize are just trying to make sense of the nonsense. Or their analysis, labels, and categorizations are feeble attempts at self-justification. I realize these two statements are both generalizations. I am guilty of both self-justification and rationalizing nonsense. Allow me to further condemn myself by sharing my own interpretation of the human condition. There are three types of people: those afraid to die, those not afraid to die, and those too unconscious to recognize their own fear or our inevitable ascent toward death.

I wonder why the Christians fight so hard to avoid the heaven they have spent the whole of their lives trying to access. I question too why those who believe in reincarnation, like the Hindus, concern themselves with grief of passing when they are assured a brand new taut form after they cross over. Or how the pessimistic atheists cling so tightly to a withering decrepit old body? Now here is a group which wins either way. If wrong, some deity will extend the holiest virtue of forgiveness and one will arrive in some version of paradise. If right, the atheist gets to rot in the ground of self-righteousness, a maggot buffet.

I am not afraid to die. The majority of my childhood was spent trying to stay alive and at some point I realized it just was not worth so much effort. I have also held the hands of loved ones as they traveled beyond this place. Death has the potential for beauty.

Loving is a lot like dying. Both are transformative. At a core level, we are attempting to attract love and avoid death. We may even be trying to avoid death through the bonds of loving. In fact research has proven neglected infants, lacking sufficient human connection and affection, can die. In so many ways, love is a life-and-death matter.

Remember Nat King Cole's meaning of life in the lyrics, "The greatest thing you'll ever learn, is just to love, and be loved in return." It is a basic assumption we all want to live and be loved. I want that as well, and I want something beyond love. I want an honest life. I want most to live without masking, altering, or hiding. The realization of a life which has been fully lived, hinges on telling the truth, it is the chief tenet of authenticity.

The truth is, Vince avoids me. We used to go to bed together, now he stays up late. And when he talks, I find myself not listening. Our conversations have been reduced to the normal marital chatter… kids and work. We do not talk about Thomas. Secretly he is hoping he will die, and die soon.

When I poke at the anger associated with being nudged away, my carefully prepared meals ignored, I realize the sadness I am feeling has been buried for a long time. I, too, fell for the naïve fairy tale. I believed in the possibility he could be my knight in shining armor, rescuing me, nurturing me, and protecting me "through good times and in bad."

Now I am approaching my forties and I realize the knight and shining armor image is a fantasy contrived by Mr. Walt Disney in a brilliant attempt to fill box offices and bank accounts without regard for the fragile nature of relationships and the human attachment to illusion. I can give up the dream of a rescue, but nurtured and protected feel like a life-and-death matter to me.

Vince and I stopped fitting together. It is not his fault. We both love each other immensely. If I were to leave him, he thinks he would die. He has spent all of our marriage trying to be perfect, trying to give me what I want so I will not leave and he will not die. The new toys, completed projects, and stock options are nice, and of little importance now. I do not want stuff, I do not want perfect, I do not want to always get my way. I want honest. And I want an authentic life, however messy, complicated, or painful.

Not long ago I found one of my journals from my early thirties. My birthday wish list to my husband read:

More French kissing
Dates together
Caresses
Laughter
Attention
A playmate
Connection

Occasionally one of those wishes would be granted. On most days I was content. Unfortunately, the seed of separation has been planted. I watered it with a forbidden love affair, and Vince fertilized it with long hours at the office.

I am lonely in my marriage. Still, tonight I will press my naked body against my husband, my breasts touching his back, my knees in the crook of his legs. I will listen to the rhythm of his breath and feel how when he is turned away from me I can still try to make us fit.

Like I said, I am not afraid of dying.

BROWNIES

Not unexpected. Whatever limits Josephine chooses to explore, there will always be one more ante to pay.

On this spring weekend retreat at the beach house, she's anxious to share a pot brownie a friend slid her during a birthday gathering. It's been eons for both of us, and brownies, a first—far too long to have any memory or sense of where it'll lead. Our worlds are all about kids, soccer practices, fitness routines, marital disconnections, bills, contract negotiations, scheduling conflicts, and carpet spots left by the dog.

Josephine loves to explore, and when she reveals the small brownie, she is smiling like a giddy schoolgirl. She hands me the larger portion, not even a full bite. I can smell the marijuana. We chew together—another adventure on the high seas. She returns to the kitchen to gather the dinner while I gather wood for a fire.

Then she appears just before dusk with a vinaigrette salad and a white pizza cooked on the grill. We dine on the picnic table lit by a lantern. I have never tasted pizza so good. The crust crunchy, the cheese soft, green chilies the perfect contrast to the sweet tomatoes and grilled chicken. Josephine sips a Chardonnay, me a beer, and we watch the waning evening against the horizon, hues turning to violet and shadows casting themselves on the ocean. And far out on the water, a lightning storm playfully reflects against the distant waves.

My fingers graze her thigh as I breathe the scent of her hair and kiss her cheek. Us again. We are apart from the entire world and together where we belong.

Feeling the early release, I offer, “If this is the view I’ve been missing…I really need to start getting high.” She laughs and we kiss for what seems like hours, her tongue so yielding and wet, so pure and ready.

Then we talk and laugh and hold hands and watch the night fold in beyond the fire. Josephine shares a recent experience at a music festival. She embarks on a winding tale that truly fixes my attention. The bands, she says, are all cover bands and perform in full imitations of the Beatles, the Rolling Stones, Aerosmith, and Prince. She describes the side show performers, jugglers, fire breathers, and a most incredible sword-swallowing act. I sit riveted as she tells of the final demonstration when the assistant pushes the sword deep into the performer’s throat. She abruptly stops, and with a casual sigh discloses, “Not really. I just made the last part up.”

I pause suspended in disbelief, then we both break out in uncontrollable laughter. Beautiful Josephine. At last I reach to guide her back into the warmth of our bed, I feel her pull, a second’s hesitation. In her sudden resistance, I hear her whisper, “I’m waiting for a question.” My mind reels. What question?

How could she question the depth of my devotion? Thoughts ticked away in the turn of seconds. “I’m already in—what else is left to question?” Until suddenly I understand, the one forbidden question she is seeking. She just wants to hear me ask her to marry me again. I see it in her timid glance, her vulnerable yearning. I want to ask her, I need to know, too, and so I ask, “What will your answer be?”

She doesn’t hesitate, only leans into whisper, “My ass.”

A moment’s silence follows while I considered her answer. I can’t even imagine the question she had in mind. It doesn’t matter. We collapse to the floor in pot-infused fits of laughter. My stomach aches as I desperately try to catch my breath. Another moment of perfection.

The moment we finally enter the cottage we are gripped with the pot-high munchies. Josephine is too elegant for Cheetos or Ding Dongs. She pulls a white narrow box of Almond Thins from the grocery basket. Oh, my God. Never has there been a more sublime gift to the tongue, all sensations climaxing together, candlelight, the rhythmic crunching, the taste hinting of caramel. We eat them one by one until each thin is devoured and the package exhausted. She sits quietly a moment, as if pondering the meaning of life before asking "Well...shall we snort the crumbs?"

I nearly fall from the bed in an explosion of laughter before she calmly adds, "In the future, remind me any and all brownie experiences must include a sizable cache of low-calorie snacks. Like the broccoli and celery sort where you burn more calories chewing."

CHAPTER TWENTY-ONE

With our children in school and our spouses at work, Thomas picks me up from my home. We drive to a hotel, it is always a new place. I wonder how many more years it will take before we run out of hotels. He had a business meeting in the afternoon and he promised to leave me bound and tied to the bed until his return.

Upon our arrival, I slip off his tie and unbutton his shirt, medium starched and royal blue to match the color of his eyes. I put my arms through the sleeves and even with the cuffs rolled up, the arms cover my wrists. We make love with me still in his shirt. Long gone is the awkwardness of our first encounters. Thomas has memorized my body. He reads my thoughts even before I do.

The previous week was spent away with my family. Thomas, now lying next to me naked, kisses my cheek and neck. I whisper for him to tell me a secret.

He confesses, "When you are away I turn off my cell phone because I cannot bear to see a call come in and know it will not be from you."

He tells me I have surprised him once again. Usually when I come back from a holiday with my family or a trip with my husband, I call off our affair.

Smiling I say, "I considered it, but after all this time I've finally come to know my path, and it always leads back to you." Since his diagnosis I have allowed no other man into my life.

When Thomas leaves for his meeting he is wearing his blue wrinkled shirt and grinning. My sinuses are congested from a cold so he orders me to rest and forgoes the ropes. He leaves me lying there bare eating red raspberries and drinking sparkling water. Some reality show is on the television. I wonder where I was when the world turned mad. Then I remember I was in the arms of my pirate captain.

To the question of whether a marriage can sustain an affair as mine, I wager the answer is no. Although on most days, I hope it can. To the question of love, not the ideal type, the real painful beautiful kind I have to come to know inside of a marriage and outside it, too, the answer is clear—a person cannot thrive without love.

Even if she could, why would she make that choice? I am not big on sentiment yet I have reached the conclusion people are willing to sacrifice so much for even the slightest chance at love because it is oxygen to the soul. Love also holds the greatest potential for heart ache. To love is to leave your underbelly fully exposed. Love is a brave choice.

Two hours later, Thomas returns. I am napping beneath the sheets. He undresses and crawls into bed next to me. His hands move over me and inside of me naturally. I awaken to him. I hear a sound and it is my own voice purring with the rhythm of his breath. When he whispers, "Now come for me," my body answers his command releasing the warm juices to flow between us.

I do not know what is to come or what will be. I only know what exists in this moment. In the beginning I built a castle. The walls were strong and made of carefully crafted stone. I tended the kingdom until one day the rain came. I looked upon my castle and realized the mortar I had used was made of sugar and dreams. I stood and watched it crumble with both sadness and joy because now I want to build something new.

Something without walls...like a sky...the color of royal blue.

THE CASTLE CRUMBLES

January 18th

Exquisite Josephine,

You know, I get the feeling you just don't need THIS right now. I really want to be a source of strength and support rather than adding to your confusion. While my own desires get in the way sometimes—I hope you can see the truth of my heart. If then, my feelings complicate, if I make your road more difficult, your vision less clear, or your future less sure, then I have no real choice but to step aside.

I've made my feelings about us and about you clear. I also want you to realize I can put my needs aside, if they are holding you back or tearing you asunder.

There's no pressure, timeline, demand, or ultimatum here. I'm beside you no matter what. I always will be. What I care most about is you. If you call, if you need me, I'll be there. If you decide to stay, if you decide to run away...I'll be there. In an instant or a year, I'll be there...wherever this journey leads.

What I know is how much I love you. What I know for certain is circumstances will never change my devotion to you. If this is where we need to be, then I will accept that, too. It won't change my love. Sometimes I still sink and retreat into myself because I don't trust what's coming.

Sometimes I want to give up. I remember you and all we share and all I learn...and then I recall, anything is possible when you trust and let go.

If, in these silences, if you think I will fail you—you're wrong. This is an important time, for you and for me. I know the insights we most need couldn't come any other way.

Whatever the future holds, I won't stop loving you.

Thomas

CHAPTER TWENTY-TWO

I left my husband. It was not something I planned, not consciously anyway. We spent December together, Vince saves his vacation time and takes off the entire month. I had promised myself I would appreciate our time together and work our way back towards intimacy. I tried to be present, affirming, and available. After a month of intentional misses, I arranged for a date night and we spent the last evening at dinner and a movie.

Distance was the only thing we shared and I couldn't even remember when we had stopped making love many months earlier. The connection was gone, the conversation empty. I look back now and begin to realize there were other indications.

During the summer I had committed to a strict budget so within a year we could be completely debt-free, excluding the mortgage. I began to learn things, things I did not understand: the sprinklers, online bill paying, changing the furnace filter, turning off the water on a leaking pipe.

My soul knew before my head acknowledged it. By the time the final evening rolled around, I was long gone. It was dramatic at first.

"Our marriage is over, Vince," the first words lingering in the air as the car pulled into the driveway. He did not believe me initially, the too familiar tantrum, perhaps. My anger escalated and I stormed up the stairs and began tossing clothing, a toothbrush, and make-up into an overnight bag. Anger, however, was not the emotion I could sustain.

By the time he came into our bedroom, I collected myself, "No, we're not going about it this way. I'm not storming off in the middle of the night. I have loved you for the last two decades and I will love you for the rest of my life."

Instead, I undressed and crawled into bed. When he came to me later in an attempt to comfort me or change my mind, I was sobbing. "Please, Vince," I cried, "We can't continue this way, I want to honor you and I want you to stop punishing me. It's time we let go."

He tried to convince me I didn't mean it. Before leaving my bedside he mumbled something about "working it out." In the morning, he was there in bed, lying next to me just like he had been for the last twenty years.

I realize it is a lot to ask of someone to share something they love, especially a wife. Still I really love Vince. Marriage is not something you bring to an end. Once you share yourself intimately, your heart, your soul, your genes, you are eternally bound.

I took our two daughters to breakfast and explained there would be some changes. I told them in a too-brief-way their father and I were going to live separately for a year. We held each other and cried.

My youngest took it pretty hard. She is fiercely independent. Even as a little girl she insisted on going places by herself like walking her sister to the bus stop and taking letters to the mail box. When she was about to turn five, she begged me to walk the perimeter of the park behind our house, alone. It is about the length of four linear blocks. I agreed on the condition she take the dog with her. I did not want to impede her courage and willingness to take risks, but I also felt fiercely protective. So I watched her as she turned the corner out of sight and then I climbed out on the roof and tracked her every step of the way, as best I could.

I too was eager for my own independence. I tried to reassure the kids their lives would remain the same. My favorite aunt says, "I have a way of painting rainbows over reality." It is not meant to be a compliment. It would take me years to fully acknowledge the weight of my decision to leave and how it would forever change our children.

Our families never saw the separation coming. No one did. I sincerely thought once you had found peace within yourself, external conditions were irrelevant. I was wrong. Context does matter. Our lifestyle choices have to align with our internal evolutions or we experience great discomfort and discord.

I am not stupid, I always knew having one foot in two different places was unfair to both my husband and my lover. Gradually, without conscious realization, my feet had repositioned themselves, together, in a different place. At some point in my marriage, and I am not sure exactly when smiling across the table at each other and kissing goodbye became somewhat of a lie. It may sound crazy, I refused to accept some sanitary pretense as a substitute for what had once been a beautiful union. Vince would have tolerated my love affair; I wanted to honor Vince and I wanted to honor myself, too.

When the choice came between keeping my family together or following the soul's longings, I chose what I knew was most right for me. It is selfish, I recognize this. Still, I felt there were enough times, years, in fact, when the needs and desires of my children and husband were placed first. There is integrity in living your truth. At least this is the story I tell myself in the doubt-filled darkness of some nights. We are all trying to find ourselves, and our way, those paths at times cross in beautiful union and other times in violent collision.

Throughout the initial transition, Vince and I proved we could not only do marriage differently, we could do separation differently, too. We had conversations, the kind that lay you open and leave you raw. Vince wrapped himself in a blanket of denial. I wrapped myself in a blanket the color of crimson, fully prepared to do the difficult grief work. It did not come, not at first anyway. I waited for the tears, instead came full breaths of relief.

I spent the next month planning the logistics. Vince and I agreed to focus our attention on the girls and make the decisions which would best serve their interests. It took some time to make new living arrangements. I negotiated renting a room at my Aunt's house just a couple of miles away. Vince moved into his childhood home, which happened to be sitting vacant.

Vince was scheduled to be on travel for a week at the end of the month. The plan was for us to begin living separately when he returned. It seemed the best way to facilitate a smooth transition. To preserve their sense of stability and security, our daughters stayed in the house while their dad and I rotated back and forth. Because my work schedule was flexible, I spent weekdays in the family home and Vince returned to stay with our children on the weekends while I was at my Aunt's.

The necessary preparations were made and we helped each other get set up in our new places. I worried about him. Did he have enough towels, was his bed comfortable, would he eat breakfast? He worried about me. Did I have Internet access, was there cable (I never watch television), would I have enough money?

Thomas graciously took a step back during these changes. I needed some time to process the new arrangement. It was too easy to direct any resentment at him and too easy to run to the safety of his arms. When blame was the convenient emotion, he was the nearest target. When fear overcame me, he was the easier escape. So the two of us created some time and space, believing it was only temporary.

The irony is the difficult times in our love affair began when I ended my marriage. Desmond Tutu says we need relationships to teach us about humanity. He is correct. And sometimes solitude can teach us about ourselves. I have been in a relationship since I was a child. I had moved from a bedroom in my father's home to live with Vince. There was something I missed from never living alone, it is in the quiet where we learn the smaller inner voice that is our own.

When the moving day arrived, I pulled a card from "My Course in Miracles" deck, it read, "Everything you teach you are learning. Teach only love, and learn that love is yours and you are love."

My car was loaded with a few remaining clothes and the meals I had prepared for the weekend. I wanted to spare my children the painful sight of watching us pack so most of the moving was arranged while they were at school or away with friends. On the Friday of the first weekend I was to live separately from my family, my oldest was having a sleepover at her friend's house. Vince had just returned from the airport, he looked drained and exhausted. We had invited a close friend of our daughter's over for a play date and to serve as a distraction.

The moment I remember most clearly is saying goodbye to my youngest daughter. She was sitting on her bed, the tears welled up in her eyes, puffy and red, and bearing a strained expression of distress I had never seen before. Suddenly I realized it was a mistake to have invited her friend. This was a scene that never should have been witnessed, not by anyone, not even my daughter. My baby looked so small, curled inward, frightened. I held her, feeling the wails shutter throughout her body, making their way to the surface disguised as whimpers. She was trying very hard to compose herself, to be strong. I could feel her anguish so acutely and suddenly I wavered on the choice to leave.

This was not a brave choice. This would not be a lesson of love. The course I was teaching, was loss.

THE DECISION

It began as a simple afternoon. I haven't seen Josephine in a while and I miss her madly. She and Vince are struggling. I like Vince, I really do. He's a great guy. I can't nearly fathom the depth of love allowing him to accept my bond with Josephine. It's incredible really. Sarah could no more do that than fly to the moon. So for once, stepping away and allowing Jo to address her needs, was my idea. We've caused enough grief.

Instead, I spend my time trying to get back to some kind of normalcy. I clean the garage, get to the gym more for workouts, focus on coaching the kids' teams, and get caught up on work. She is there though, always there, in my thoughts and in my heart. I miss our easy laughter. I miss our daily conversations about life. I miss the depth of our connection. I miss the smell of her hair when she cuddles up to me. I miss feeling her release into surrender when she's in my arms and the affirmation she never allows herself to fully let go otherwise.

In this space and distance, even Sarah and I are getting along. We've shared so much together over a twenty-five-year marriage, but the elephant remains there, right in the middle of the living room, enormous and looming. I have to walk around the damn thing every time I walk in the door. We share a kind of love for each other; it's not the same as it was in the beginning. It is the love of a longtime friend and parenting partner. It is not intimate, or passionate, or soulful, still it is there. Long, deep resentments unspoken are held on both sides and have grown too large to overcome.

I remember in the beginning, how much I wanted to share with her about the connection I was experiencing with Josephine. Crazy thought. I really did though. I thought it would be remarkable to have the kind of relationship where you could tell each other anything. If only we lived in such a world —Josephine's world.

Sarah is not Vince, and I'm not so naive to think there would be anything but pain, and grieving, and wrath. The devastation would be immense. And so through all these years, I've said nothing. I walled off a most important section of my life; protected it with fortified defenses. I began to see the possibility I had led the elephant into our home. Was it me who solidified our descent? I couldn't imagine how to rectify it or make it right. Maybe there was a way, but I sure couldn't see how.

As the sun set on our simple afternoon and I played in the yard with the kids, Sarah cooked dinner, watching us from the kitchen window. Here amid a beautiful reality my cell phone began vibrating in my pocket. It was Josephine. She was sobbing. Could I meet her somewhere now, "Right now?"

"Of course." Always. Forever.

I raced to the familiar parking lot with a knot in my stomach. She was hurting. Something was wrong. I'd do anything to keep Josephine from suffering. When she pulled beside me, I looked across at her. Her expression was flat, still, I could see she'd been crying. She got out of the car and into the passenger seat. She made no attempt to crawl into my lap, as she always did. I could read something in her eyes…what I couldn't tell. She made one single statement. "I've left Vince."

I felt, I swear to God, I felt like I'd been hit by lightning—a thousand volts of electricity. The hair stood up on my neck. I studied her mouth in disbelief. Of all the things she could ever say, it was the last thing I ever expected to hear. I don't know why it came as such a shock. It is a familiar progression to many affairs. In fact, the possibility of a life lived together was the deepest yearning of my heart for so long there was no way to recall when I had first fantasized about it—even before we were ever together. There it was and I never saw it coming.

Josephine had always been open with Vince, and he with her. They shared honestly with an unconditional commitment to communicate that I could never understand or hope to achieve. They had the kind of authentic relationship other couples envied. And it wasn't until now I could conceive of the real possibility Josephine would leave her marriage.

I felt too many emotions at once; I couldn't breathe. My first thought was my marriage is over. The moment was here. Finally, we were going to be together in the open daylight. I was ecstatic. I wanted to kiss her, hold her, and laugh out loud. I wanted to shout, "I love you so much!" But I was choking on the guilt. I felt a deep remorse for Sarah and Vince, a soulful recognition of the pain we already had caused and would continue to cause.

I was afraid, afraid to finally face Sarah with the truth knowing the imminent destruction, the bottomless, heart-rending anguish of broken trust and betrayal I was about to hand over to her. And the kids...the shattering of their secure dream world. I was angry at myself for all of the losses looming on the horizon, the family and friends who would all be impacted. That feeling was replaced with hopeful optimism, joy, and the thrill of possibility. All washed over with the feelings of sadness, and then immense terror, and self-loathing, and again love.

CHAPTER TWENTY-THREE

In every story there is a shedding of self, an emergence of a new being perhaps more enlightened. I apologize if this does not happen here on these pages. In the beginning I was a lover, a mother, and a child. I still am. I am not on my way to becoming. I will always be her:

Brave and afraid
Silent and loud
Compassionate and selfish
Insightful and silly
Evolved and small

I make no excuses for her, for me. My only real success in life is I have failed at being anyone else.

Thomas is asleep next to me. I have been lying here listening to his breathing. Feeling the slight tickle of his hairs as his chest rises and falls. I cannot recall a time since we began sharing a bed, when I have been awake to watch him sleep. I wonder if it signifies something...a change or a new beginning. It is unlikely. Soon he will wake up and dress himself, returning home to a darkened house and the family who pretends not to notice he has gone missing...again. Like you I am waiting to find out the conclusion of this story, where it leads and how it ends.

Thomas and I went out earlier tonight, and for the first time we began to feel like a legitimate couple. As we begin openly cavorting, introductions feel awkward. "Boyfriend" sounds so twelve-year-

old. I finally settled on the introduction, "This is my man, Thomas." I have never used the title before and it somehow felt appropriate.

Still, one older woman asked, "How long have you been married?"

Thomas answers boldly, "We're not married, we are together."

She blushes and reminds herself to stop asking that question. "I sometimes forget the difference between the centuries," she says smiling.

He flashes his reassuring smile in return. I have gotten over the blank space formerly occupied by my wedding ring. I do not even notice anymore when I am out with my children and someone recognizes the lack of a gold band. So much of a women's identity is wrapped up in family. At the party, a more recent friend of mine asks, "So how long have you known each other?"

"We can't remember when we first met," Thomas answers. Then I chime in, "...About thirteen years."

She gets a puzzled look on her face.

I lean in and say, "It's not a pretty story, hopefully just a pretty ending."

Another friend adds, "Isn't that true about life?"

As the party comes to a close, Thomas leaves me at the banquet entrance while he goes to get the car. Standing there my phone vibrates. It is Thomas. He has texted me the words, "Damn, you are beautiful."

I smile and wait for him to bring the car around. I think back on the previous four years: the year of e-mails and phone calls; the year of falling in love and making love; the year of living before dying; the year of not dying. We have now entered the fifth year of our story, the year of choosing.

We return to my little room at my Aunt's house. Before I can finish brushing my teeth, he has stripped off his clothes and is waiting expectantly under the down comforter. I make up my mind not to make love to him this time. After all, he is the man my mother warned me about, the one who will say and do anything for the keys to your coveted temple. I undress slowly and he watches me. He lifts the covers for me and I have every intention of falling right to sleep.

Then he looks into my eyes. He runs his hands over my backside and along my thighs. He caresses me while avoiding my feminine parts. He handles all creases and every bend as if he were discovering me for the first time. I am caught in his gaze until I can resist no longer. My body craves him. I move my hips forward rhythmically to the song playing only for us. His hands loosen my knees from one another, and his eyes examine the moistened folds with gratitude and appreciation. He is no longer a visitor to this temple.

Then he makes love to me the way he always makes love to me, like I have been his from the beginning of time. My resolutions and defenses collapse like water droplets in the desert. I give in to the moment...to the madness...to the magic. The endless meaningless chatter of the world is once again replaced by the quiet of our breathing.

In this instant, the right now, I feel myself carried off. Detached from every tomorrow and absent of all the yesterdays. It is only temporary. In the morning I will go back and force myself to remember the "where-I've-been's," the "what-I've-learned's," and the dwindling memory of who I was then. Because tomorrow is always different. I get so busy meeting the new me, I sometimes forget the old one, and how I do love them both.

In his dreams beside me, Thomas tastes the saltiness of the waves splashing against the side of our ship. I am laid out on the bow, bathing naked in the sun's rays. The power of the ocean bears us forward and the sky opens before us mixing with sunshine and promise.

COWARDICE

Cowardice is a field rabbit, scampering zig-zag over the next hill at the first sign of trouble. All you see is a flash of feet and tail. This is my response to all conflict. I try to avoid anger at any cost. It's fucked up. It's passive-aggressive sometimes and at other times just full-out denial. It is the kind of defense which allows hurt and frustration to grow into insurmountable walls. It is the Achilles' heel of every relationship I've ever had.

Relationships, by their very nature, broil with conflict. Clearly, I lack the necessary tools. So I did what I always do. What I had always done. I hid and lied.

I did not leave Sarah. My intentions were clear. I knew my marriage was over years earlier, I simply could not imagine living apart from my boys. There it was my indefensible standard choice, I will not walk away, at least not until the safety of night when my acts of treason can be concealed by the darkness.

I will sleep in the basement through eternity, if that's what it takes, but I won't take responsibility. I'll just sit here in the corner like an angry child and glare out at you. I will be so difficult and so removed I will force you to make the decision I, myself, am not capable of making. It will be left to you to alter the destiny of four lives forever—even though the choice was already made years before without your consent. God forbid I face the hurt, the anger, or the destruction borne from my decisions to lie and cheat.

At the first hint of fire, Josephine walks resolutely toward the smoke and right into the flame. She cannot abide passive or passive-aggressive. She approaches the uncomfortable parts of life from the direct side, while I attempt to scramble over the hill, or worse tunnel underground. Josephine looks you in the eye. She faces the truth in all its ugliness.

She's fine with loss and pain. She's made friends with anger and hostility, as long as they are honest. The truth is all she asks. While I have to marshal all of my resources to look back into those eyes and resolve to abandon the old patterns to hide. And I am so tired of hiding…

When the time comes to tell Sarah, my throat closes off and the words are dry clumps wedged in my esophagus. The boys are asleep. Sarah's senses are on full alert, her eyes brace her for the declaration she has been avoiding. She fills the room with small talk, trying to engage me in a line of questions I cannot hear. I'm thinking intently, "How do I fit the word 'divorce' in between carpools and teacher conferences?" When I finally utter her name, "Sarah," she looks at me and smiles gently.

"I'm sorry," I stutter… "I'm so tired."

"Goodnight," she calls as the basement door closes behind me.

CHAPTER TWENTY-FOUR

So here it is, the ugly part. The part I did not want to tell you. This is where Thomas leaves his wife. Where he tells her he is filing for divorce and they will have to sell their house. The same house he roofed, painted, landscaped, remodeled, maintained, and raised his children in for the last fourteen years of their lives. And this is where she begs him not to leave. This is the part where she threatens to take everything including his kids. Here is where she cries and pleads and says it is all her fault. And where she screams and yells and says he is to blame.

She left him long before I came into the picture. She did what most American women do after cleaning toilets, preparing meals, and folding their one-millionth load of laundry, resent their men. So she pretended not to notice when he would wink at her. She declined his advances and turned away from his embrace. With the help of a few glasses of wine she slept soundly each night with her two children and her two-car garage and the husband who helped dream it all, asleep in the basement.

Then one day, he was gone. Suddenly, she could not remember why she hated him. All she wanted was for him to hold her again and to tell her how her little piece of illusion would not change and she could go on pretending all the stuff made her happy and safe.

Thomas spent countless evenings consoling her, having the open and raw conversations Vince and I had six months earlier. She wanted him to move slower and I wanted him to move faster. He said, "Josephine, this takes time, compassion, understanding."

My tone, cold and dark, "The reason you came to me was because you were miserable in your marriage!"

I vividly remember the night I left Vince. Guilt was not part of what I was feeling. I wonder about the differences in my head trash. Am I missing the compassion chromosome? Did I skip the lesson on loyalty? Or, is Thomas still trapped in his little boy head looking for approval? Is he still earning the certificate that says, "I'm a good guy and so I deserve to be loved." I really cannot tell who is fucked up here.

Sarah is the victim in this story…this is the reminder I give myself tonight while lying in bed alone. I try to be patient. Another phone call is endured. "She's falling apart, I can't come tonight." Thomas apologizes profusely.

I answer, "Save it. I don't need coddling. I'm not interested in joining your list of disappointees so you can indulge this cycle of self-deprecation." I have no desire to fulfill his father's claim, real or imagined, of "the son's failure saga." Guilt does not absolve and neither does the self-administered castigation. Eventually you have to just walk away from both.

On our good days, I hold my pirate captain lover and tell him he is not going to make everyone happy and some things cannot be fixed. Men are so fucking arrogant, like they have the goddamn power to heal our wounds and mend our cuts. He still believes he can, which is why he stays. He says, "I don't want my sons to be afraid or to not feel safe."

I ask, "Have you been able to prevent them from feeling afraid all these years?"

"No." He says, "But I've been there when they did, and now I won't be anymore."

He is right. I verbally give him permission to stay. Of course, I want him for myself, I just know it to be the right thing to say. In fact, for the first time I hate his kindness. Oh, irony must love me. Here I was the one to resist, the one to run away so many times. Here I am now trapped in a silly love triangle, my lover comforting his bereaved wife and me not able to sleep away from him.

On a dark night very soon children will cry themselves to sleep.

A woman will pick her broken dream up from the floor and stoically walk herself to a marital bed left empty. I am sorry. I so much wanted to write to you of a beautiful love story.

THESE ARMS

I don't have many memories of childhood. The entire hard drive was wiped out somewhere along the way, with the exception of the most traumatic. Sometimes, still, I ponder whether the ability to remember marks the difference between functional upbringings versus the alternatives the rest of us face. My own memories were erased for a myriad of fairly valid reasons, survival greatest among them. When a child of four or five is faced with these kinds of choices, selective memory can be the cornerstone for what is catalogued as retrievable.

What is unforgettable is anger can escalate quickly, a father choking a mother out on the living room floor and blackening her eyes until she runs screaming into the night, leaving her crying child behind. What is remembered is being beaten by the devout Deacon, crumbling to the garage floor, you feel his righteousness increasing with each kick of the boot to your stomach, until you can no longer breathe. The memory retrieved is the trusted Christian youth pastor who slides his hands into a young boy's jeans. There are but a few memories.

While such circumstances fall outside this story, they are integral to how I came to the place of not being able to move forward and not wanting to turn back.

I loved Sarah. I did. I couldn't leave because I wanted more than anything to be an example to my boys. The example of a different, all-loving, and perfectly capable father, ensuring my children the security I never had.

When Sarah finally feels herself backed into the corner and rages at my leaving the dirty dishes in the sink, knowing full well she meant my dirty affair in the middle of our family room, I cowardly tell her I want a divorce.

She won't stop crying. She says she wants the answers…she "thinks" she wants the answers. Offered are the gentle white-washed versions she can package up and file in the place where pain and disappointment make sense and have order. The truth in this case is far worse than any story she'll make up and I unfairly leave most of it to her imagination.

I want to protect her, I do, just to offer some comfort to salve her wounds, only I'm the knife. I let her set the imaginary timeline…the summer…enough time to transition to her new career. Of course she requested a therapist, of course I obliged. Suddenly there were home-cooked dinners. At bedtime she would step out of the bathroom in satin camisoles, her libido magically reignited.

I didn't tell Josephine, there were nights I made love to my wife, not out of guilt—I can manage the guilt. Heartbreak is a whole other proposition. I did it because making love seemed like a better goodbye than walking out the door, and because I'm a coward.

Night after night of the lengthy discussions and tearful pleas, Jo waited. When I felt she would wait no more and I had sufficiently backed her into a corner, I left Sarah. I looked into the eyes of my wife and partner, the mother of my children and the girl who had shared the dream from the beginning. The girl I had once chosen to share it all with. I looked into her eyes, and then I walked out the door forever.

CHAPTER TWENTY-FIVE

It is winter again. Thomas is still in his family home waiting for it to sell. We have fallen somewhat into our own routine. We have a date night one night during the weekend and spend the following day bicycling, walking the park, riding the motorcycle, or making love all day, depending on the weather. We have our coffee and tea on Sunday mornings and all seems well. On this winter's eve under a full moon we have joined our friends, six other couples, to snowshoe up a nearby glacier and then retire to a nearby resort and a warm jacuzzi.

After dinner we drive to the parking lot at the foot of the glacier and gear up with gloves and mittens. Thomas is a sweetie securing my snowshoe mountings and carrying the pack of water and emergency heat packs. We begin our ascent trudging through the snow, the moon directing our path through the woods. I keep checking on him and his tender heart. "How are you doing?" I ask. Then I hear myself sounding like a mother hen and after my last, "Are you okay?" I tease, "You are excellent, I know," winking, "I've had you."

It is incredibly light here. My boots and snow shoes move in rhythm across the hard-packed snow. Eventually we are beyond the trees and stretched out before us is only white. The incline now is so steep, we can only take a few steps before having to stop and catch our breath. The sky is a pitch-blue contrast to the white peak and we are nestled there between the light and dark…always. With our eyes cast forward we continue until we are halfway up the glacier.

It is amazing and empowering to me how our actions and exer-

tions, however small, lead to progress. I want to hike to the very top of the mountain, but I can hear Thomas panting. I try to pace myself to match his starts and stops. When we get to our friends, Mike and Candace, we rest and are joined by two other couples. The rest are ahead of us intent on reaching the peak. Mike announces, "Well, this is as far as I go."

"Me, too," says Candace. "I'm freezing."

I turn to Thomas, "What do you want to do, babe? Shall we keep going or head back down the mountain?"

"You call it," he says, "Whatever you decide..."

I take this as a signal he is tiring. After the last couple reaches us, we turn to head back down the mountain. I discover the snow is slippery and I can slide down instead of hiking. I lean back on my down jacket and begin the slide downhill, my snowshoes pointed forward in the air. To stop I stab my poles in the snow. Others join me. We are laughing hysterically careening down the mountain, human sleds. When I look back, I do not see Thomas.

"Where's Thomas?" I shout.

"He went ahead," Candace shouts back.

"Alone?"

"Yes, he said he was going to climb to the top to meet with the others."

I am in utter disbelief, grateful my expression is hidden in the collar of my parka, my anger buried underneath my hat. I scream all of the way down the mountain...in my head. Thankfully I have some time to collect my thoughts and process the chain of events before my reaction runs away with me.

I am standing off the trail when Thomas comes clomping along with the second group. By now I remember when anger is expressed, Thomas interprets it as criticism and he retreats to his faraway shame place where he is unreachable. I also recall a conflict communication technique I learned years earlier at a marriage retreat I attended with Vince.

When ___________________happens,
I feel________________________________
It reminds me of __________________________________
Please (and thequest)_____________________________

In the calmest voice I can muster I say, "Babe, I really wanted to go to the top of the glacier, too. When I asked what you wanted to do, you said, 'Whatever you want, we'll do.' When you left me, I felt very alone and it triggered my fear of abandonment. This was really something I hoped we would do together. Would you please communicate with me?"

He is defensive. "I called after you, you didn't hear me. At the last minute I decided I really wanted to go to the top."

"I did, too," I snap.

Then I turn and head off in the direction of the others to avoid being left behind a second time. When we get back to our cars and trucks, I take off my gear and silently climb in the front seat. I know Candace is cold and I am also anxious to get out of the elements and back to a more private setting.

The car ride down the mountain is painfully silent. Despite my best attempts, Thomas has gone to the shame place and I hate him for this. I am the one who has been wounded and he is playing the victim. Our dysfunctional childhoods hamper mature adult conflict resolution, and once again we are children stomping our fists and throwing tantrums. My little girl joins little-boy-Thomas.

"Why don't you just drive me back to my place!"

Silence.

I want him out of the shame place and in the car with me communicating thoughts and feelings like a functional adult. So I say the stupidest thing possible, "I'm done with this…done with you. I really tried to handle this misunderstanding in an honest and gentle way. I knew you would be defensive, and I really tried to communicate so you could hear me. The one instruction we were given on this trip was not to go off alone. Still you left me. If you are determined to do everything alone, then go ahead be alone."

Silence.

Little Josephina emerges in a full scale rage. She is red faced and sprawled on the floor twisting in fits, pounding her limbs, and spitting anger, further wounded by his unresponsiveness, "Just drop me off. I'll get a ride home. I can't even stand a car ride home with you."

We pull in the parking lot and he grabs my gear and storms into our room. I pass him in the hallway as he goes out to get another load. I am taking off my ski pants and boots when he throws my duffel on the floor. The door is open and he begins shouting.

"Fine, if you want me to leave, I'll leave. The little princess didn't get her way and so you end it. Everything I do, I do to make you happy. You know what, there's just no winning."

"Shhh," I whisper, mortified. "I don't want anyone to hear us fighting."

This only seems to encourage him. He shouts louder, "I do everything I can to take care of you and you allow no room for mistakes..."

I crawl under the covers and pull the bedspread over my head. This may be the first time Thomas has ever yelled at me. The door slams behind him and I am left alone in the dark.

I scan my body to check what I am feeling. In my chest there is not the shallow breathing of sadness. There are no muscles tight with anger. There is only quiet and the slow drain of adrenaline.

I call my girlfriend Amanda. We talk through the events. I call Thomas. His voicemail automatically answers.

"Thomas, I want to apologize for telling you it is over. I didn't mean to say those words. I was angry. I know you really work to make me happy, and when mistakes are made, you get triggered. I know it is important for you to try to please me. I do love you and I even expect mistakes will be made on both sides. And, I am wishing you could see the little girl inside of me, the one who is feeling hurt and alone and instead of defending or protecting yourself, needs you to put your arms around her and offer comfort and reassurance. Instead of growing silent, I would have liked for you to say, 'I'm sorry I left you. I wish I would have known you wanted to hike to the top, too. We belong together and I love you.'"

Then I hang up the phone and fall sound asleep. In the morning Amanda picks me up and drives me back home. I have a message from Vince. He called wondering how my snowshoes ended up on the front porch and wondering if I was okay. I am getting really tired of this story.

THE LIES WE BELIEVE AND THE TRUTHS WE MAKE UP

I really want to sort this out. I really don't want to repeat the mistakes of my past. Two days later I listen to Josephine's voicemail, six times.

I'm trying to understand this latest breakdown so I can learn and get better. Obviously I'm not good at the anger thing. This is my issue and I've recognized more and more over the last few years how anger plays out in my life. I own that. It's not a shame thing, just the recognition I handle blame horribly.

I wasn't in the best place from the beginning of the snowshoe trip. I was already tired, the day was stressing me out, I was scrambling to get ready, my son was pissing me off, and I felt like I was upsetting Josephine because I was wavering on where and how to meet. That all may not have necessarily been a factor other than by the time we headed up the mountain, I was spent.

And then, it just felt to me like the perfect storm. I didn't anticipate her anger, and when she let me know, our friends were standing there listening, ready to move on. Her words were completely healthy and reasonable, and I didn't want to make a scene by having a heated discussion in the middle of the trail with everyone standing by with their headlights directed at us. When she sat in the car without talking to anybody, I thought "Oh, no, here we go. I fucked up, and just like Sarah, she's gonna make sure I pay."

I'm learning this kind of assumption is my own shit. I don't know how, yet I honestly want to find a way to understand when Josephine is mad, what she really feels is hurt, and what she really needs is a hug and reassurance. I wish I had the gene to help make me understand how sometimes when a woman is angry and pushing away, she is actually asking to be drawn in close, to reestablish the connection. It totally confuses me when she says, "I don't want to sleep with you or see you anymore," and what she is actually meaning to convey is, "Please hold me, I'm frightened and I want to be with you." Wow. Just wow!

God, how I wish women came with an instructional guide written in the male language. I clearly don't have the skills to interpret the expressed communication as something being implied entirely differently. Despite my issues, I believed Josephine when she asked me to go away and she didn't want to see me anymore. Important note to women: We do hear you and we trust the words you speak. Try to speak clearly and say what you actually mean.

That night I was so angry because Josephine seemed so willing to throw all we've gone through away the second I fucked up. I feel like I dote on her. I try to spoil her at every turn and the minute I don't act in accordance with the expectations, she tosses me aside.

What can I say? When she pulls away, I still fear the future without her. When I'm this tired, I can't find the words to explain or reassure. I feel like I don't have the resources to be myself. I am so afraid of losing her.

I don't trust the words out of my mouth, so I write:

Josephine,

After all this time…when will you just trust?

Why does true intimacy always cause you to challenge and distance and push away?

I've long since accepted the timeless importance of this path,

and our love.
If I screw up, when I screw up, I want you to forgive me.
When you get scared, I want you to run to my arms.
When you are in doubt, I want you to believe in me and our connection.
I'm sorry I hurt you. I should not have left you.
We have together challenged, sacrificed, and risked everything for this course.
I believe in this path. I will not abandon you, no matter what the future brings.
Please forgive me.

CHAPTER TWENTY-SIX

I went away for the weekend; traveled to the dark place within, the lonely places where you look for yourself. It took some searching, when I found her...me, I finally asked the question. "Are you running from fear or towards freedom?"

Thomas was supposed to spend the weekend with me. Only his schedule kept growing shorter and shorter. First we planned for two nights then he could only make one. I could feel his resistance. The divorce papers have been submitted, still he and his wife are living under the same roof. At first I said I would not see him until he had moved out, then at the last minute his roommate arrangement fell through and I could not endure another month-long separation. So I caved. I can see he is really struggling. I am, too.

For much of my life I have not trusted in romantic love. My earlier examples of relationships showed more disappointment than fulfillment. In many cases being alone is easier because you have all the control. Looking back, I see now how my relationships lacked intimacy because I always kept open an escape hatch and a few extra safety nets. Most of this is connected to the experience of abandonment in my childhood. My father left me, my mom, and younger brother every two or three years. Usually other women were involved, sometimes he just left. My mother left us, too, with more frequency. Her lover was a vodka bottle and she never came back the same. No matter how hard we try, those childhood experiences create an imprint. Whatever work you do, there is no denying those early introductions to the world and the human experience.

In my own marriage, I worked to stay separate and then condemned my husband for his absence. It has taken me a long time to make sense of things, through all of this I have learned to forgive humanity, especially myself. Thomas asked me to trust, and I have. Even though he is not here now, I trust him, I trust our love.

For my part, I have upheld the contract. Thomas is learning detachment. All along I expected it was me he would have to let go. It turned out to be everything else that mattered in his life. Like Siddhartha who laid down his worldly possessions or the monastic who take the vow of poverty and celibacy, we have both had to turn away from the materialistic, idealistic, cut loose our security nets, and close our exit hatches.

We have plunged into the abyss of uncertainty, the realm of intangible. What we are finding on the other side is not each other, we are finding ourselves. Before you can love someone else unconditionally, you must first accept yourself. Love is a spiritual journey. Only through self-awareness, acceptance, and connection to something bigger than yourself can you experience what love is, how to give it and equally how to receive it.

Thomas for many years has pursued me. I have resisted, evaded, and run away entirely. I had work to do, work of the spiritual nature. I am here, though, now. My emergency exits closed, my safeties released. I do not know where Thomas is…lost in some battle. He is not where he promised he would be.

I am disappointed. My current struggle is to not internalize this transition, not associate this progression with the old childhood experiences of abandonment. His grieving process is not a personal rejection, even if it feels that way.

I must sit at a distance and watch my partner as he bids farewell to his earthly attachments…wife, home, investments, and identity. Just as he has watched me lean into surrender and stand bare in this new place of vulnerability. We are growing and it is dark and light, glorious and sad, painful and rewarding. This must be what surrender looks like…

Christmas is coming. At this cottage by myself I drink tea, read, take walks alone on the beach, and long naps nestled in layers of blankets, warmed by the sun. I'm realizing, I am not afraid anymore and I will always search out the path to freedom, welcoming the next adventure, with my partner or alone.

EXIT HATCH ENGAGED

This should have been the most beautiful love story. It really should have been. At the time, I couldn't have believed in anything more strongly. Josephine was my refuge, my life, and all my dreams come true. I couldn't have wished for anything more. Through her, with her, I experienced what it was like to live in the moment and feel truly alive in the world.

Except…her world was not my world. I had attached myself too completely to the role of husband and father. My marriage, children, the four-bedroom house, and two-car-garage had been my illusions, too. It all offered me a sort of protection. The doctorate, the business, the half-million-dollar home—I had accumulated the evidence of self-worth. With everything gone, I didn't know what I had left to give. I didn't even know who I was. Or maybe I did, maybe that was the problem.

And so began the slow, tedious process of separating myself from Josephine, separating myself from everyone close to me and beginning down the path of self-destruction born of guilt and shame.

Each time I took off one of my masks, the face underneath was not visible. I tried to distinguish the man I so wanted to be. I looked for the lines and the details that would now define me. Beneath the emptiness was more emptiness with no way to transcend. So I looked for an escape, an escape from the past, an escape from who I had become.

Escape has a myriad of confused and twisted forms. For me, the path of escape turned out to be alcohol. What a demon. It didn't happen overnight. It took months and months, a gradual step-by-step collapse. It allowed me to forget the devastation, and God damn, how I wanted to forget.

So I drank a little more, and then a little more, and then a bit more. I drank until I could no longer control it, and then I kept drinking. I drank until the beauty of the romance could no longer sustain itself, right into the point where the new story of self-destruction was complete. I drank until I could no longer remember why or how I had chosen the journey in the first place.

Honestly, I couldn't remember anything anymore.

CHAPTER TWENTY-SEVEN

Today is my birthday. My girlfriend Nicole and I are in a hot springs in New Mexico. It is a magical little spot in the center of nowhere. Painted red toes break the surface of the water, my body rests buoyant in the mineral pool, my mind is heavy with Thomas.

I am trying not to count down the days until his divorce is final. He has finally moved out. The house he is renting is a mile from his home and he shares it with two other bachelors.

His little brother came into town. At first Thomas wanted him to meet me. Then the feelings of failure crept in again and he hesitated. I asked, "Thomas, in all these years we've been together, your brother has never come to town. So when do you think he'll be back again? How long before this opportunity presents itself a second time?"

We decided to play it by ear, to wait and see how the conversation flowed. Late Thursday night Thomas called me. I was in a pair of sweats and slippers headed to my weekend abode. He and his brother were at a dive nearby playing pool. I threw on some jeans and applied some mascara, blush, and lip gloss. Teeth brushed and perfumed I drove to meet them.

It was disastrous. Not because of the brother, I liked him. He was similar to Thomas with an overbearing physical presence balanced perfectly with a tender heart. He was a gentleman and I could tell he loved what his brother loved, and it did not matter what I said or how I looked. One of Thomas's friends was there, too. I had heard about Nick. Thomas had mentored him throughout his youth and was a surrogate father of sorts. Nick did not take the news of the divorce well. He told Thomas, "We are men of honor. I look up to you, and men of honor do not leave their wives."

The youth in every generation are a contradiction of principled naiveté and rebellious disorder. Thomas had not told Nick about me. Throughout the entire evening I sat next to Thomas without being able to touch him and listened to Nick tell stories about Thomas' soon-to-be ex-wife. With the insecurity from our recent distance and still decades away from my own full maturity, I engaged in a "big dick contest" with young Nick.

The poor guy had prided himself as the champion of insults. I have long since learned the banter of boys is the way to determine positions in the power structure. My background in Mediterranean culture, alcoholic dysfunction, and politics had left my edges filed to a thin blade. I have yet to meet my match in the arena of serious debate or witty banter. I can assess a person's weaknesses instantly, and I am an artist when it comes to exposing contradiction and inconsistency. So while pompous Nick lashed wildly, each jeer was met with precise sharpness. Of course, I emerged the victor, smarter, funnier, and with the bigger dick, despite having only a vagina.

I hated myself. It was as if I had watched the entire heinous scene from some distant place while the internal screams to "stop" fell silent against the roar of the unchecked ego's heartbreak. I wanted Thomas to put an end to the miserable tragedy, to take my hand and Nick's, too, and assure us both it would be alright. I so badly wanted him to give his confident smile, letting us know we would be able to keep our principles and our dignity. He sat silently drinking beer after beer. Removed. Only offering the occasional chuckle at a well-landed jab.

When the bartender shouted last call, the shells of ourselves gathered our things to go. I said goodbye to his little brother. Thomas was going to drop him off at their mother's house and meet me back at his place. I wanted to drive home. I wanted to leave this scene of carnage and catastrophe. I wanted to step out of my role as mistress or girlfriend and drive off screen. I have done it before. It is the fa-

miliar course.

I love Thomas. So this time I resisted the urge to run. I understood it would be difficult to create a new life together. I recognized there would be anger, sadness, and judgment. Nick was a shadow of the discomfort yet to come. I wanted to wrap myself around Thomas. Together, I knew we could endure the consequence of our actions.

When he returned to his bachelor pad, I was there waiting. Knowing his triggers, I chose my words carefully. Reaching out to touch his shoulder, I assured him. "You have done nothing wrong, this is not your fault. Tonight was incredibly difficult. To hear Nick talk about Sarah hurt more than I thought it would."

"Oh, baby," he said, his hand reaching out, caressing my leg. It was the response I had hoped for. The air I had been holding in my lungs found release and I buried my face and tears in his chest. I undressed and our naked bodies huddled together, temporarily protected from the harsh realities of expectation and disappointment. In the darkness we had managed to find refuge and each other. I drifted off into a gin and tonic slumber.

Only when I woke up again a couple of hours later, Thomas was gone. I listened in the darkness. I could not hear any noise. I thought he must be in the bathroom. So I waited for him to return. Minutes later the door cracked open and a stream of light broke through the black.

I called out to the light in the hallway, "Where did you go?" My answer was the click of the door handle closing shut. This time, I heard him go into the kitchen. It was too much to bear the darkness alone. My old fears seeped into the crevices of my fragile psyche. My own vulnerabilities around abandonment took hold.

This was the time I needed desperately for Thomas to hold me. I knew better than to lash out and push him away again and yet the fear I felt was so acute I could not lay still next to his empty spot. I dressed. I walked quietly down the stairs. I did not turn my head. I could feel him standing in the kitchen as I passed.

At the front door, I paused to put on my boots and find my keys. He came to stand beside me. He did not speak. I did not look up. There was only quiet and the faint beating of two very distant hearts. One word...one touch...something...anything to tether me to him.

I felt alone with the burden of love and loss. I felt his retreat with every cell in my body yet could not speak the words, "Please, Thomas, do not let me go." All I could feel in the moment was loneliness. It was too much. As he stood there, stone silent, I stepped outside into the last vestiges of winter and pulled the door closed behind me.

Today is Sunday, it has been three days since the night with Nick and my solo drive home in the snow. Tomorrow my birthday will be over. Thomas will not return my phone calls. He does not answer my texts. I am floating here on the mineral seas beneath a desert moon waiting for my pirate captain to return to me.

SILENCE

CHAPTER TWENTY-EIGHT

It is Tuesday now. Yesterday I returned from New Mexico. There is still no word from Thomas. I have been feeling his withdrawal for months now. At the bar and during his brother's visit, absence had checked in.

Each time I call and it goes to voice mail, or another text goes unanswered, my heart sends a message to my brain in a language incomprehensible. How can he completely shut me out? Where would he go? Why would he leave? My own wounds are too great to stop him, unable to coax him to the together place.

Nicole spent the entire weekend trying to reassure me and then distract me. She has suffered her own romantic losses and we commiserated over the challenge of allowing ourselves to love knowing it comes with the certainty of some degree of suffering. She reassured me, "He just needs time, Jo."

"It has been more than five years," I remind her.

"Yes, and there is a finality to divorce. This is a very emotional time for everyone. He is dealing with the pain and loss of his children and family members, as well as his own. He will come around," she tries to assure me.

I am sick with fear and grief. There is a boulder sitting on my chest and I literally cannot breathe.

I have tried everything to shake the panic, meditation, miles of crawl stroke in the lap pool, yoga, long hikes, and finally one of Nicole's Tylenol PMs. I am exhausted and unable to sleep.

I have even toyed with the idea of letting go. My intentions are powerful, I can manifest just about anything so I was careful in my wishing. I could have wished to be over and done with Thomas, I did not. I could have wished for him to run back to me, I did not. Instead, I wished for peace and understanding. I know what I want, I do not trust what I need.

In a moment of complete frustration I drove over to Thomas's house late last night. His roommate told me how he had moved out over the weekend. Am I trapped in an episode of the Twilight Zone? I fear I may finally be crossing over the edge to crazy.

Next, I drove by his home, the one where his wife and kids still live. His car was not in the driveway. I knew he was not there; I parked outside a few houses down and waited anyway. Seven minutes later I drove home sobbing, helpless and feeling humiliated. This is not me.

When I woke in the morning, I could not make out the sentences my children spoke as they readied for school. When I got to work, the words on my computer screen all ran together. My thoughts are hijacked by my emotions and I cannot seem to hold onto a single idea. I feel like someone hit the pause button and I am moving in slow motion. Driving to a meeting I could not get out of and still completely out of my mind, I finally asked, "What is this?"

Pain, was the answer.

"This pain feels greater than me," I thought.

Then by merely naming it, the agony retreated. A rainbow did not appear, although my senses reengaged and I began to see and hear again. When I was about eleven years old, I contracted a severe case of mononucleosis. I did not leave my house for weeks. The doctors kept diagnosing me with strep throat, the antibiotics only made me worse. My fevers would average 103 degrees.

After seven days straight of being trapped in my own bed by delusions, I called for the end of my suffering. My father heard me groaning as he came in to rub down my sore muscles with isopropyl alcohol and lower my temperature with ice packs. He comforted me between my body aches and hallucinations. "Josephine," he called through the haze, "Welcome the pain. Invite it in as if it were your friend."

Because I was so far away from reality and so tired of struggling, I followed what seemed like impossible instructions. Relief came immediately. I learned in the most physical way, it is the struggle to avoid and deny our pain, not the pain itself, which causes the difficulty. Resistance expands pain.

So here it is. I feel totally abandoned by Thomas. I admit, I refused to trust him in the beginning, yet the moment I committed myself to his promise of devoted love, my deepest fears were realized. I gave him my heart and he has rejected me.

This is the secret to pain. Once you invite it in, you are able to examine it more clearly, see it for what it is. Across from me sits my pain, this is not new, it is an old pain with origins from my very beginnings as a child.

For more than four decades I have been protecting myself against abandonment, rejection, and loss. I have avoided intimacy because it left me vulnerable and unprotected. What I began to understand in this moment my pain joined me for tea, is that I was reliving an old story. The characters were different, the story was still the same. The man I needed, the man I loved, had left me alone.

I sat in the car, outside of the meeting I was supposed to be joining, and thought of all the ways I had tried to prevent any chance of abandonment. How I had chosen a husband who was defined by loyalty. How after years of marriage, I had sought new lovers to provide affirmation and validation. How I had kept my distance from Thomas for so long, guarding a fragile and frightened heart.

To abate the possibility of loss or withdrawal, I would maintain several relationships. At the first sign of difficulty, I would end the relationship before risking disappointment or rejection. I had left Thomas again and again. And, I had left my husband, too. Looking back over my past failed relationships, I could not recall a single romance or friendship where I had not exited the relationship.

In my longing for Thomas and grappling with the uncertainty of our future, I began to taste the bitterness of my own medicine. I had split so many times and been the first to leave so many people. Every time I would feel afraid or get angry, I would gather my things, trust, affection, friendship, and slip out the back door. The thing I had been calling detachment for all of these years was fear. All along I had been running from the fear of loving and losing too much.

Instantly I began to see recent events very differently...the scene in the car where I had told Thomas I was done...walking out in the middle of the night. Then I remembered Vince and all of the leaving, physically and emotionally. I text Vince before running into my meeting, a new veil lifted.

The following morning Vince meets me at a coffee shop near our home. We used to share the same side of the table, now he sits opposite from me. He smiles and makes idle conversation because he is first and foremost polite. I listen for the resentment in his voice, it is simply not there. Our conversations differ only slightly from when we shared a home and a bed.

I stir the honey into my tea and wait for the letters to attach into words in my head. It was never my intention to hurt Vince. Now my own heart lay in pieces, and for the first time I understood intentions have very little to do with outcomes. So I took responsibility for the pain I had caused this good and gentle man. I owned the pieces of his broken heart, the shards bearing my name.

I wait for a break in the conversation, "I've asked you here so I can apologize." The tears well up in my eyes before I can get the last word out.

He smiles tenderly, "Josephine, this isn't necessary."

He's worried that if the pain is named, it becomes more real. He may be right, suffering holds its own spell and naming the pain is the beginning to breaking the spell.

Vince takes another sip of his coffee. He would rather be anywhere else than having this conversation. I have to ask myself, "Who will this apology really serve?"

Reassuring myself this is for his benefit, I continue. "You have been really good to me over all these years. Especially during this separation. The tears spill over, "I want to thank you for loving me so completely and unconditionally."

He softens around the eyes and I catch a glimpse of the pain he is trying so fiercely to deny. Occasionally, friends or family would ask,

"What does Vince think?"

I always replied, "I have no idea."

Even after twenty years together, I still had no idea how he felt. Once I found a diary and reading it was like being introduced to a stranger. There was a rage and hostility, I had never witnessed. When I asked him about it, he answered, "Jo, those words were never meant for you. I simply needed a place to vent."

I remember whispering my response like it were a wish, "I would have liked to have known that part of you…I would have liked to have known all of the parts of you."

My parents were checked out and I married a man who was emotionally checked out, too. He was preoccupied with work and deeply committed to routine. He avoided any uncomfortable feelings through a systematic process of denial, still, he was consistent and reliable, and so I felt safe. Safer in fact, than I had ever felt before. I was allowed complete autonomy with minimal expectations and zero limitations. Together, with the partnership of a very kind and caring man, I was able to heal many of the wounds from my childhood.

The part missing with Vince was a deeper sense of intimacy. If I wanted to uncover his feelings, I had to push the envelope to elicit an emotional response. Threatening to leave always did the trick.

The truth was I had repeated my parents' story, the same story that had wounded me. I protected myself, and the little girl inside who was left behind, by doing the leaving. The book, Getting the Love You Want, written by Harvel Hendrix, details this relationship dynamic. I had read it years earlier, but until now, I had not fully grasped the significance in my own life.

With the light filtering in through the coffee shop window, I look squarely into Vince's pain, "I'm sorry. I didn't honor you the way you deserved to be honored."

He shifts in his seat, allowing me to continue. "You're an extraordinary man, Vince. It's after this distance, I can fully appreciate you. I really wished I would have set a better example for our daughters. You offered me both freedom and security. I took too much for granted. I took you for granted."

"I thought if I gave you your autonomy, you wouldn't leave," he whispers.

I am offered a small glimpse...

We sit in the silence for a moment, allowing the words to sink inside of us to the injured parts deep within, "The betrayal was so unfair, I'm so sorry for leaving and the hurt I have caused you."

His hands rest folded on the table and I want to touch him. I want to wrap my arms around him and erase the ugliness. To go there would only cause him further harm.

"We both made mistakes," he says. The politeness having left him.

I want to ask about his mistakes. Not because I want an apology, rather so I could better understand all of this, too. That line of questioning would only shift the focus away and the least I can give him is this single moment of repentance.

"Whatever stories you tell yourself, Vince. Please know this. I was wrong to entertain a relationship with another man. I was wrong to leave our marriage. If there is a way I could make amends for the pain I have created...."

We used to have this process for when one of us screwed up. If either of us made a mistake, we would follow with an amends, a simple recognition of our error and an acknowledgment of our partner's feelings. It was the responsibility of the receiver to accept the apology and make a request for restorative justice so the forgiveness process could be complete.

Once I accidentally backed into Vince's car in the garage. That was a lot of blow jobs. Both his mom and dad kept asking him what had happened to his car. He never told them it was me. Eventually when it would come up, he and I would laugh.

He was notoriously late from work while the children and I sat at the dinner table waiting, steaming right along with the asparagus and lemon grilled Halibut. If dinner delays and cold bites of food had not happened so frequently, I may have found more enjoyment in the back massages and chocolate chip cookies, baked especially for me, with more walnuts and fewer chocolate chips.

While tucked away in the booth, I was hoping Vince would make an amends request so we could complete the forgiveness process. A request would have selfishly absolved me. I knew my transgressions were much bigger than any possible amends could offer. Some things cannot be restored, only endured.

As we began to gather our things to leave, Vince reaches out his hand to touch mine, "Thank you for the apology, Jo. I know you love me. The love is the only part I remember."

THE ELUSIVE TRUTH

The more Josephine tried to paint a beautiful future together, the more broken I felt. Her honest conversations made me want to jump out of the window face-first after having doused myself in gasoline and lit myself on fire.

I kept telling myself I was trying to protect everyone—Sarah, my boys, Josephine. The ego within kept trying to justify my behavior, I knew though, the soul knows. I had compromised Sarah and my sons to get what I wanted, what I thought I needed.

The "I" had superseded the "We." Everything and everyone had been so compromised, the landscape read only of destruction. I could only look out over the bloodied fields of carnage and pour myself another Scotch. Reclamation requires honesty, but I was buried ten feet under in alcohol-induced oblivion trying to dig myself free.

Occasionally the numbness would wear off and I would briefly entertain the ego thoughts, "I can take care of everything and everyone." Then my memory would reengage and I would be left with the image of cardboard moving boxes and the tear stained faces of my sons.

Before I could bring the glass to my lips, the real and made-up voices hiding in the deepest recesses would whisper, "Look what you have become." So I would drink longer and faster, until the warm blankness would wash over me leaving the quiet hum of dissolve.

CHAPTER TWENTY-NINE

It has been a couple of months since my birthday. Thomas and I have been talking occasionally, even though we have not seen each other since the winter night I walked out. It is Friday night, the weekend. My children are with their father again and I have nowhere to be other than out with my girlfriends. We choose a trendy restaurant downtown for dinner and drinks. Spring is in full swing and the natives have emerged from their winter solace.

Nicole is sitting across from me. She is single. She too has little patience for mankind's imperfections. Her father did not love her enough and we share a familiar shield of protection. Illiana is sitting next to me. She is a contradiction of strength and vulnerability. Her husband left her with a two-year-old while she was seven months pregnant. She wants him back. Her arm rests naturally against mine, a shared sadness nestles between us.

Together the three of us sit on mahogany benches eating salads and drinking vodka tonics. Actually, mine is tonic, while Illiana takes her vodka straight up. Nicole is on some diet with a bunch of letters that do not spell anything. Her glass is filled with iced tea. She is strangely animated tonight, stealing quick breaths in between hurried sentences. I might like her better drunk. "How long is this diet?" I ask swallowing a mouthful of arugula, pears, and goat cheese.

My cell phone sits next to me in case I need to answer a text message from Thomas. It is totally rude to be out with friends and texting your boyfriend. Tonight I do not care.

Nearly three hours later when our conversations of literature, politics, religion, mothers, and men have all reached their conclusions, we pay our check and head off in separate directions. I text Thomas I am leaving.

"Come and see me," he writes.

"Ask me nicely."

"Please, my love, will you come over so I can spank that sweet little ass of yours?"

I turn in the direction of his new place. He has moved in with a longtime friend of his, Jill. On my way he texts again, "Jill says she can't be responsible for what comes out of her mouth."

"I'll see you some other time, then," I write, after pulling over on the side of the road.

"Perfect. Goodnight," reads his sarcastic reply.

So I call him and in the calmest voice I can muster, I explain, "Thomas, I am very fragile right now. I cannot endure the rejection and denigration from one more of your friends. Maybe it just isn't a good night."

"Jo, it is fine. I want you to come over. I shouldn't have been flippant with my comment. I just wanted to warn you, Jill also went out with friends. She's been drinking all night. She just ended a romantic relationship with her girlfriend, and she's not in the best condition."

I should have trusted my instincts and driven home. The lure of this man is so great. He assures me he just wants to be together. It has been so long...I go to him.

The introduction in the living room is short. I pet Jill's yellow lab and compliment her on her beautiful home. She replies, "You are beautiful."

There is something in her voice making it sound unlike a compliment. Underneath her smile is a sour tone, the kind that smells of sulfur and leaves a metal taste in your mouth.

I am trying to decide what's behind the resentment when she offers us a drink, I politely decline, "No, thank you. I've met my two-drink limit, it's late, and I've got to get up early."

When she steps into the kitchen, Thomas nods for me to follow him. He leads me by the hand into his new room. It is much nicer than his first bachelor pad. Light oak floors replace nylon carpets. His new bed has a headboard and more fluffy pillows than a straight man knows what to do with. I encouraged him to rent his own place, yet every time we looked at a condo or a town home, I could feel his resistance. Looking around at Jill's, I understood. He could not go from his home filled with children's chatter and hordes of family paraphernalia to an empty apartment alone.

Our reintroduction feels awkward. I thought back to a phone conversation the week earlier. I had asked him what he did during those five days around my birthday when he refused to speak to me. He explained how he and Jill had reconnected. They used to work together years earlier and shared a close bond. She had offered the extra room at her place and he needed the support of long-time friend. After he moved his things in they sat on the back porch for hours drinking beer and catching up on each other's lives. "I just confessed everything I was thinking and feeling over the past five years."

It was the first time he had told anyone our whole story. Listening to him I became so angry that while he was cutting me off, he was seeking comfort with Jill. I screamed into a pillow. My oldest daughter knocked on my bedroom door asking if everything was okay.

"I'm having a moment, dear…just working through a bit of frustration. It's okay. I'm okay.".. Although I had worked through my fit of rage, all of the sadness and disappointment over the last few months has left us both spent.

Standing in this unfamiliar room, there is a distance between us, a separation growing increasingly more familiar. He does not undress me as was our usual practice. I so badly want to feel my skin next to his. Eventually we both remove our clothing and settle into our proverbial curve. I think, "If I just feel his heartbeat next to mine, perhaps we can be synchronized again."

As we both breathe in our first sigh, Jill begins to yell, "Thomas! Thomas! Josephine! Come out here. You've got to see this!" referencing something on the television.

Thomas climbs out of bed immediately. In the middle of her next sentence, Jill's tone shifts to slurring hostility. "This is my house!

I'm not going to have this! She is not going to disrespect me."

I hear Thomas's muffled whisper followed by complete silence. I listen for quarreling, nothing... I wonder, "Do I go out there and talk to her? Do I wait here? Do I get up and leave again?" I was about to pick the latter when Thomas returns.

"Oh, my God," he says. "Is there anything else that can go wrong in our lives?"

"What should I do?" I ask in a state of total confusion.

"Please don't leave," he pleads. "I just want to rest with you."

"What's her problem?" "Am I the enemy?"

He pulls me into his arms, "She's just being protective and her problem is too much booze."

I stay. We sleep, stealing whatever reprieve is offered from our worn-out hearts. Between intermittent dreams we grasp for the vestiges of a sanctuary lying desecrated. In the morning we both wake early and tiptoe past Jill's door to our morning destinations. Thomas has a baseball game to coach and I, the "sacrilegious soccer mom," have a game to cheer.

Later in the day we talk, and I offer to try again with Jill on neutral ground and under better circumstances. I mention a place called the Old Tavern.

He says, "Possibly."

He calls me early evening to say he wants to save the meeting with Jill for another time. "I just need to be alone with you. I'm going to get a hotel so we can be together without any disruptions or distractions."

I have already made plans to have dinner with a friend, so I say, "Call me when you are done putting your sons to bed."

At 10:20 p.m. when I am past ready to leave Candace and Mike's, I text Thomas.

"You are not waiting for me are you?"

10:26 "Not for long."

10:27 "What does that mean?" The words betraying me already, "Where are you?"

10:35 "Where are you?" comes the delayed response.

10:36 I call Thomas. There is no answer. I text: "Please call me.

I've been waiting for you. I don't understand what is happening."

No response. No call. No text.

10:42 I say goodbye to Candace and climb in my car. On the way down the road I call again. No answer. The tears begin filling my eyes, distorting the road in front of me. I hope for a cliff up ahead. I call again. No answer.

Then I lose it. I leave a message on Thomas's voicemail. There is no way he can understand what I am saying through all of the crying. I stop making sense anyway. Frantic, I drive toward Vince's house, our house. It is fifteen miles closer than the place where I am staying temporarily while I wait for the short sale on a condo to be finalized. I recognize the downward spiral I am descending and need a familiar place.

Vince is already asleep, he picks up my call right away. He cannot hear me through my sobbing, either.

"Do you need me to come and get you?" he asks.

"No," I mutter.

"Josephine, I can't understand you. Come here, come home, it will be okay," he says. After all the hurt I have caused him, he says, "Come home."

The bedroom light is on. I am crying so hard Vince is unable to figure out what has happened. I show him the text messages, he still does not make sense of it.

"I don't get it," I cry. "He was supposed to call me and we were going to meet."

Then I speak the words very clearly in a voice completely still, "Vince, I'm concerned for my own safety. I feel as though I may try to hurt myself. I'm drowning here and I feel so utterly hopeless."

"You need some rest," he says. "In the morning this will not feel the same."

I shut off my phone and close my eyes to the darkness.

DELIRIUM

What followed is a blur to me, a lost time. It was a complete period of numbness and confusion, where the direction was so unclear at times I simply let go of the rudder and drifted. I couldn't seem to remember myself or Josephine.

It was supposed to be the best of times, liberating, freeing, and stepping into dreams so long anticipated, the time when our love would be championed. I kept asking myself, "Why am I doing this?" "Why does the earth keep crumbling under my feet?" "Why am I walling off my heart?"

Nothing was as it should be, and the moments became bittersweet and tragic until there was nothing left.

I waited for Josephine at the Tavern on a red vinyl bar stool. Smoking had been banned a decade earlier, while memories of a crowded bar, the smell of cigarette ends glowing, and the juke box playing in the background remained. The bartender dried glasses, ear bent towards a regular patron retelling a story for what had appeared to be the fiftieth time.

My plan was to meet Josephine for a drink and make love all night at a nearby hotel. I can't get my bearings. It's her scent, the smell of her breath, the softness of her skin, the wetness of her lips—I so badly want to remember who I am and why I'm here.

Her text comes in as the bartender pours my fourth beer and I've already forgotten. Everything. What a long, long way to travel…to be so lost.

CHAPTER THIRTY

The morning did not come for me. Not on this day. Vince handles my outbursts the way he always handles my outbursts, which is to ignore them. In the morning I find myself perched in the bleachers of a lacrosse tournament with him whispering something into my ear about the parent to the left. I turned to him and said, "Do you remember me telling you I wanted to kill myself?"

"Yes," he said, "Of course. I just thought you might like to talk about something different."

"Call my aunt, please. She'll know what to do." My aunt is a social worker.

When we get home, I climb the stairs, pull the covers over my head, and wait for help to arrive. It never comes. An hour passes and then another hour. Downstairs I hear movement, footsteps and voices. I call my aunt myself. It is the rarest of occasions when she does not answer. I dial my best friend, Amanda, expecting to leave a message, she never picks up her phone.

"Hello," she answers.

"I'm in trouble," my voice cracks.

"Where are you?" she asks. "I'm on my way."

Fifteen minutes later she pulls up in my driveway and five minutes afterwards I am loaded into her Suburban and heading east. I say, "If I could just get through the next couple of days, I think I could be all right."

I have so little energy, my voice is barely a whisper and each sentence is spoken as a question, "Right now in this space, I don't know how to get through the next minute? I might need to be committed to a psych hospital and put on suicide watch?"

I explain how I do not want to bear this one incident of desperation for the rest of my life on my medical record, yet I sincerely do not want to wake up tomorrow.

By this time, the lifelessness has already established itself. I can barely even speak. Through broken sentences I tell her what happened on Friday night at Jill's. Then I explain how we were supposed to meet after Thomas put his kids to bed on Saturday. How the text messages made no sense to me. How loving Thomas has become so painful I cannot bear it a moment longer. She pulls into a hotel parking lot and goes inside. When she returns, she helps me out of the car and gently guides me to a neutrally decorated hotel room.

There is a queen-size bed, a sitting room with a sofa, and a small kitchenette. I have little memory of the twenty-four hours as I alternated between Ambien and Demerol. The Demerol was left over from my foot surgery. The bottle read, "Take as needed for pain." So I did.

I took several baths, my body completely submerged in the warmth. Only my nose was left to mingle with the outside world, vaguely a tendril left to connect me to the living. I floated in the liquid warmth, my body scarcely tethered to my soul.

In the evening I had something to eat, I can't seem to remember what. Amanda was a saint. She never left her post. She sat quietly in the sitting area while I slept. If I was awake, I was crying. She brought me tea, pressed a cold washcloth to my forehead, and rocked me like a child.

Never in all of my years have I ever felt so despondent. I am far more intellectual than emotional. My response to challenges is to process cognitively exercising my cerebral aptitude. Emotions are not to be trusted, they are temporal and dynamic. I have been able to analyze and synthesize the most dysfunctional, insane, and absurd experiences. In all my capacities, I could not understand what has happened between Thomas and me.

We had fallen in love. We had eliminated the barriers in order to spend a life together. I ended my marriage. He ended his. We thought the path would be cleared, instead we lay amid the shambles of two broken families and could not find our way back to one another. It had become a nightmare. Real or imagined, I did not want to wake from a situation I could not think my way through, and the emotional roller coaster had simply become too great to bear.

So I slept in a drug-induced fog while Amanda watched over me. There in the darkness I found other guides pointing me toward flashes of light. I quit thinking and I settled into the sadness taking residence in the softness of my belly, and the frustration gripping hold of my hands and twisting them into unrecognizable fists. I felt the grief with each exhale, and with each inhale I prayed to find the peace within.

THE ABYSS

When Amanda called to tell me Josephine was suicidal, I didn't answer the phone and I didn't respond to her message. I had nothing to offer. If I could wave a magic wand, I would make this all okay, except everywhere I turn there is pain and sadness. I feel like I need to save myself; I haven't the slightest idea of how to even do that.

I hit bottom. These past few months I have disconnected from everything and everyone. It is honest to say I physically couldn't function because I fell to a place so dark it's literally indescribable. I have experienced depression in my life, nothing like this.

Suffering a barrage of guilt and rolling grief in waves upon waves without ceasing while days blended into nights. If there is a hell, then I have known that place. If there is an abyss of the soul, then I have walked those empty hallways. I have trodden the silent depths of my spirit. I have sunk to my knees and fallen prostrate onto the marble of the mausoleum floor, felt its cold relief upon my cheek, and prayed to dissolve into the ether. My prayer far deeper and more beseeching than any appeal to the eternal I've ever dared whisper.

In the previous six months, my company plummeted into a free fall and my income with it. I scrambled and marketed, but nothing was working. By April I was bringing in less than a quarter of what I was making the last year. The recession hit, all of the contracts dried up, and I had no way to pay the mortgage on the house, much less finance a place for me and my boys. By the time the holidays hit, I was totally under water. Creditors were calling, retirement was depleted, the IRS was preparing an audit, and the bank began proceedings to foreclose. There was nothing left.

And in the moment when I could have found my resolve, I gave up. I just gave up. I did not bother to fight back. I didn't have the strength. I just closed the door on my life. I hid every detail from Josephine, just like I had hidden every detail of my affair from Sarah. This is not the dream I envisioned. I've grown exhausted from hurting everyone and letting down the people I love most. I have failed in the most important way, protecting my children and loving Josephine. I cannot find a way out of this hell.

Once Jo asked, "Do you think you like to build things?"

"What do you mean by that question?" I replied.

She smiled tenderly, "You have a pattern of tearing things down."

I think about her question as the caramel color liquor swirls and the ice cubes make a clinking sound against the glass. All I know is I'm really tired. I sit here watching my finger pushing down on the self-destruct button and I feel powerless to stop.

CHAPTER THIRTY-ONE

When Monday came, I was surprised to see the sun come with it. Amanda had rescued me from the place of no return. She reached into the darkness, and when I did not take her hand, she felt around and catching hold of an ankle pulled me back into the dimly lit world.

Vince insisted I immediately make an appointment with Dr. Abrams, our family doctor. I told the scheduling receptionist the appointment was for an ulcer.

When the examination room door closes, Dr. Abrams, a lean, short, gentle man with thin graying hair that travels in a multitude of directions, is standing there smiling. He's been my doctor since before my daughters were born. He is the man I visit when I am sick and vulnerable. I hold a special affinity for him because he seems to be the one person on the planet that actually fixes my problems. Not always, but he certainly makes the attempt. I instantly break down at the sight of him. He wraps me in a warm hug until I can speak. I confide all of my emotional state and all of my fears.

Dr. Abrams holds my hand, patting the top with his other hand while he gently explains how if we blow out our knee, we have to treat it with medication to allow for the soft tissues to recover and heal. He recommends a low dosage of Prozac to address my "brain blow-out." He shares how half of his patients are now seeing him for mental health issues. He is finding many of the physical ailments are really rooted psychologically.

I understand. I never fill the Prozac prescription. Amanda sched-

ules me for a different appointment with the spiritual teacher we share, Anastacia.

It is the following day and Anastacia is taking me through a guided meditation. I sit on the floor and take deep cleansing breaths. Through my imagination I enter a doorway, the entrance to the earth's core. There are dark corridors leading to the center. As I walk, scenes appear on the walls. Anastacia asks me to describe the images.

I see my father lying next to a faceless mistress. I watch the shadow of my grandmother sneaking out in the middle of the night with her two daughters, one of whom is my seven-year-old mother, staring out of the back of a Greyhound bus while my half-naked drunken grandfather chases after them. One scene projects a hospital bed and my great-grandfather crushed and bleeding. A factory accident took his life and left behind my great-grandmother, Giuseppa (Josephina in Italian), and their ten children, including his favorite of all, my grandmother Angel.

I walk through the corridor observing it all, the sadness and heartache. I begin to see how the pain I am feeling is not only my own, it is also the residual disappointments, rejections, and betrayals from generations before me. I recognize how my relationship with Thomas, how all relationships, are burdened by an ancestral history.

Anastacia leads me through these experiences, not from a place of re-injury, for the first time from the opportunity to heal. In her magical, mysterious way only spirit could convey, she guides me to the mending place. Eventually I meet an elder woman. Her face is covered with a dark hood and she knows me. A large gray wolf rests at her feet. We sit facing each other for a long time speaking only with silence. When our time together is finished, she stretches out her hands to me and drops two gifts in my open palms. (Some things are not to be shared.)

I feel the fear of loss carried through the stories of my mothers before me gradually grow to a whisper. Anastacia explains how wounds, like stories, can be passed down. And healing can be passed down, too. To heal, you must first learn what ails you, you must consciously and intentionally awaken to your own pain.

Only then can you choose the right salves, select the proper dressings, and tend accordingly to the injury. If you are vigilant and persistent, the healing comes. It is then you realize we are not our wounds, or the inheritance of our past, and we have the power to write our own stories.

In the fiery center, the molten core, I leave behind the sadness of old injustices and present disappointments to burn away, I turn away from those ancestral scenes and destructive patterns and walk forward and beyond the darkness. The need to defend the wounded parts grows diminished. This will not be the way of my daughters and their daughters. I have decided to put the abandonment story behind me.

SELF-DESTRUCTION

Josephine makes the discovery on a Tuesday. We can't stay away from each other and we can't find healing together. When your foundation has been built on a lie, is there any hope for integrity in the structure?

I spend the morning repairing sprinkler heads and adding drip hoses to Josephine's garden. When things begin to fall to shit, she embarks on beautification projects. Poor girl, she so yearns for a happily ever after. How can I tell her... Instead, I cut tubing and run to the hardware store for extra drip nozzles.

Last Friday she insisted on going to the Cardiologist with me. I stepped into the bathroom just before the nurse called my name and deposited my lunch in the porcelain throne, a mass exodus in the reverse of the original direction. Back in the waiting room, Josephine reached out her hand to touch my cheek, "You are really pale." I explained I hadn't been feeling well. She interrogated Dr. Kerry about my diagnosis and the current test results.

"What does this mean long-term? Will he require surgery? Is his life expectancy going to be shorter?"

Since the doctor appointment she has been unusually silent. Josephine is the kind of woman who speaks her mind. I was simply biding my time in anticipation of the confrontation to come. You see, I hadn't really portrayed my heart diagnosis accurately. The whole episode happened at a time when Josephine had decided to end our relationship and re-commit herself fully to Vince. I recognized it immediately as the critical moment, where conflict meets the point of crisis. Faced with the possibility of losing Josephine, I grasped for any threads, anything that would hold us together.

Of course, she didn't believe me outright. She did some googling, asked to see my prescriptions and checked in with Sarah to corroborate my diagnosis. I didn't lie about the heart condition, I slightly altered the facts related to the prognosis. The details were intentionally left vague, remembering the specific words out of my mouth, "I need you, Josephine. Please don't leave."

She stayed. We lived and loved for a blissful year like our lives depended on it. In many ways, mine did. Until it was Vince she left.

Since our visit to the heart doctor, her lips stay closed when I kiss her. This morning she spent two hours at the nursery and returned with only three plants. Her eyes won't look directly at me. I'm pretty sure she knows the truth. It's just like her to calculate the gains and losses in her mind before taking any action. Her silence rings in my ears louder than any shouting.

She prepares turkey sandwiches for lunch and she looks at me and chews each bite slowly, methodically. I finally convince her to come and take a nap with me. Before I can undress her, she's climbed into bed.

When the sleep fades and my eyes focus clearly again, I notice the space next to me is empty. It's a quarter till 3:00; close to the time when her daughters return home from high school. Josephine protects her children like a wild animal protects her young, sheltering them deep inside and allowing nothing or no one to enter the inner seal of her protection. After all these years, and full knowledge of our relationship, it's still expected I leave before they arrive home from school.

I find Josephine in the garage. She approaches me holding a water bottle. "I couldn't sleep and went back outside to work in the garden."

I freeze where I'm standing, feeling the marble of the mausoleum floor beneath my feet.

"After tasting the alcohol in your water bottle, I searched your car."

She pulls two bottles of mango flavored vodka from their brown paper bags. The half-empty bottle betrays my secret.

Her voice is distant, removed, "You must have really wanted this over…you picked the one thing you knew I would not accept."

The empty hallways of the soul's abyss echo her words back in my ears, "You picked the one thing you knew I would not accept."

I'm still frozen, offering no explanation.

Josephine speaks the words with icy sharpness, slicing to the protected places I have been simultaneously guarding and avoiding. "Thomas, your boys need you. Please get help. They have already been through enough."

I feel the sinking in my knees and the beckoning of cold relief upon my cheek and my prayer returns. There is nothing I can say here in these silent depths.

I drive away as her daughters' car turns into sight and passes, oblivious to the destruction.

CHAPTER THIRTY-TWO

Have you ever looked at something for a long time...maybe even years and then asked yourself, "Why didn't I see this?" Only to realize it was your own projection obstructing the view.

I knew Thomas had lied about his heart diagnosis being life-threatening. Maybe not in the moment, however, as time wore on, I certainly had put the pieces together. As women, we know the truth about most things. We possess powerful intuitive abilities. This may explain why I was so pissed off. Honestly, I do not know how it is I could miss seeing the alcoholism.

Early on in our relationship, I wondered if he could be an alcoholic. I remember one phone call during our first year when I declined another invitation to meet him in person. He explained how after work he was going home and numbing out with a bottle of Scotch. I asked him specifically if he thought he had a problem with alcohol. His answer was emphatically, "No." Reflecting back, there were signs, signs I missed completely.

This past year of distancing explains why he was hiding from me. The only reason I thought to check his water bottle was because of a conversation I had with his mother the day before. She asked about his appointment with the cardiologist. I told her how all of his test results fell within the normal range. The doctor could not explain the symptoms I had been seeing, loss of balance, slurred speech, fatigue. When I said, "If he weren't with me, I would think he was drinking."

"He hides it," she said.

I was so shocked by her answer, I do no recall giving a reply before hanging up the phone. My analytic abilities have always served me well. Intelligence has been a source of pride for me. The thing I hated most about finding the alcohol hidden in his water bottle was being duped. It was not just Thomas, I was furious with myself. I swore I would never get involved with an alcoholic and repeat the wounds of my past. Thomas knew my position and we had this conversation several times over the past six years.

In the maze of our affair, after finalizing a divorce, losing his business to the recession and selling his home during a mortgage crisis, he had turned to alcohol as a coping mechanism.

It is hard to admit, the few times Thomas and I were together in the months before I discovered that he was an alcoholic, I could feel he was not there. Once, I remember lying next to him listening to his breathing and thinking, "I wonder how long before he will die?"

At the time, death was the only way I could imagine out of the relationship. In many ways, alcoholism is a better alternative. The power of the subconscious is it prepares you for what is ahead, despite your ability or inability to acknowledge what's coming.

In the hour of my hotel bed darkness, I dared whisper the wish to be set free. My wish had been granted. After making the discovery, I felt lighter, freer. I could finally make sense of the rubble I had been sorting through. I breathed a sigh of relief having managed to dodge a tornado. I could have been swept up in a deadly spiral obliterating everything in its path, including all of the beauty. Addiction has that result.

Initially I had taken the alcoholism personally. I spent weeks in the anger stage; rage is an exhausting emotion to sustain. I knew enough about the disease to know alcohol becomes more important than anything and everything else, which is why it is called an addiction. At times I wondered if before the alcohol, I had been Thomas' addiction.

I knew Thomas loved me, so as the shock began to wear off, I experienced new emotions...fear, loneliness, despair. At times, I so badly longed to return to Thomas, the one embrace where I felt seen and held.

With the realization our relationship was over, I stepped into a new embrace, my own suffering. I denied nothing and instead opened wide my ears to the anguish. I reminded myself of Anastacia's words, "Initially Thomas had met a deep need, and his second gift was to uncover my deep unacknowledged wounds." It would be easy to see our whole love affair as a mechanism of destruction. The thing about destruction is it makes way for renewal and a rebirth.

I commit myself wholly to the heartache. I dig out my fluffy blanket and prepare a pot of tea. I light a candle and whisper a secret prayer to find poetry in the suffering. When I am tucked in the security of my bed, I think how this has become too difficult, too spiritually taxing. I feel entirely wrung out. There is no way to bandage or deny the pain. There is only one way and it is directly through the center of the flame.

JAIL AND REHAB

It started with a trip to the county jail and ended in a visit to rehab. When the intervention came, I was already packed and ready. Josephine had called my mother, my brother, my ex-wife, and my business partner. My mother relayed the conversation in a fit of tears, “Drunk by 10:30 a.m., concealing mango vodka in a water bottle, and the immediate need for an intervention.”

Before they could organize a family meeting, I already had totaled my car and been arrested for a DUI. I hadn’t been to my office in a month, and my own sons didn’t want to see me. I was ready for rehab. Unfortunately I wasn’t ready for sobriety. That takes work.

CHAPTER THIRTY-THREE

The space created by Thomas's absence opened my life to new possibilities. I finally closed on my condo. The contractor took down a couple of walls to create space and openness. The wood floors were stripped of their old shine and renewed with a darker, richer chestnut. The kitchen cabinets were adorned with new hardware. The ceiling and walls were brightly painted.

I had imagined my life very differently, I had imagined a life with Thomas. I thought we would be sofa shopping together. At the paint store I turned expecting to get his opinions, only to remember I was standing alone. I found the perfect bistro set at a garage sale and pictured us breakfasting together in the morning air, the city skyline in one direction and the mountains opposite. At the bedding store I thought of him lying next to me, sleepy eyed with his gorgeous grin. And for every dream I had of Thomas, I let it go.

On moving day, everything was put in its place. My great grandmother's armoire newly painted white, the narrow buffet I had found for thirty percent off, a queen-size iron bed. The treasured kitchen table I had discovered on Craigslist, now in position. Thomas had first loaded it in my car long before I knew of its destination, or his. The crystal chandelier I had refurbished was gently hung. I had talked about the small-town antique auction for months. When the date came, I drove to the country alone. The chandelier was lovely, delicate and unique.

I began to create this new home for myself all on my own. You know, I liked it. It was really the first time I was living alone. I had moved in with Vince two months after my eighteenth birthday. The only time I lived on my own was my freshman year of college when I had a dorm roommate. Even then Vince and I spent every weekend together. It is strange to be halfway through your life and never have lived alone.

It was so quiet, the first couple of weekends alone in my new condo took some adjustment. My weekdays and nights were still spent with my two daughters in our family home. Vince and I arranged things so they would not have to be uprooted or shuffled back and forth between mother and father. It was not ideal, and I had come to realize "ideals," like "expectations," are things we make up in our heads.

The year had come and gone of our trial separation and without any discussion we decided to make it permanent. Occasionally we would cross paths at the house on Friday when he arrived after work. On Monday morning he would be gone again. With the weekends off, I could catch up on work, rejuvenate, and play. I crawl in my bed at night and giggle. I wake up to Nina Simone on the stereo, hot tea, and an open sky. I am at peace being alone.

Today is Sunday. My morning began with a group meditation at this super groovy co-op I joined down the street. Afterward I led a strategy session for the most amazing group of advocates working to make the world better for children and families. I had lunch at my favorite sushi restaurant alone on an outdoor patio where I instructed the waitress, "Tell the chef I like spicy and raw, please surprise me."

Then I returned home to free my bike from a hook in the bicycle room. I hopped on a new trail heading in a direction I had never been before. The unknown path opened before me, and I said "yes" at each corner.

I got home in time to shower and casually sip my iced tea while napping in the rays of the descending sun. In the evening I joined my cousins who had come to town for the weekend. We met for dinner along with my husband and daughters. When I arrived, the waitress had an Arnold-Palmer waiting. Vince winked at me and smiled. We have yet to file our own divorce papers. Our girls were refusing to talk to each other. I whispered to Vince, "What's the problem?"

Apparently our oldest daughter objected to her younger sister dating any of the boys in her grade. They are two years apart but are often confused as twins.

At 10 p.m. I crawled into my bed. Above the headboard, I had placed a new sign made of reclaimed barn wood framing red metal letters; the letters are lit with round bulbs and spell the words, "LOVE." It was my compromise for not taking red spray paint and declaring all over the bedroom walls in graffiti, "Love lives here... still." When it came to Thomas, I thought our love was unlike any other love. My mistake. Love is not special, it is common and everywhere and never-the-less, extraordinary.

Thomas' ghost did not follow me to my new condo. It was too new to bear his associations. While I still thought of him, he no longer preoccupied my every thought. Discovered is a space in between the black and white. It is the gray area. I dance there in the sadness and joy, in judgment and forgiveness, in the peace and chaos where my feet are on the ground and my heart is wide open.

SEX CLUBS AND THE RUMOR MILL

I returned home one day to find a shopping bag on the front porch with a few of my things: a pair of pants, a few shirts, three books, a pair of dress shoes, swim trunks, and a pirate's eye patch. I laughed.

It's been over a year since I've seen Josephine when she leaves a message on my voicemail. Josephine's voice—kind and relaxed.

"Hi there, stranger. I'll get right to the point, we know each other too well for small talk. I hosted a family brunch yesterday for Easter. My cousin pulled me aside and explained how his mom, my great aunt, had received a phone call. He would not identify the caller, I think you and I could safely assume the connection. Anyway, the message relayed was how I had broken up a man's marriage, a man with kids, and the word 'kids' was emphasized. The story told was that we had met at a sex club and I had seduced you away from your family.

"I collected my aunt and told them both the brief version. Yes, I had fallen in love with a man, and yes, we were both married. I told her our relationship had ended a year earlier. I said, 'The seduction part is probably fair.' It's funny, I waited for this 'accusation' since the beginning, you know all these years later, I didn't feel the need to defend myself.

"I hope you are good, Thomas. I think of you all the time, I do.

Don't feel obligated to call me back. I just wanted you to know I'm okay…it is okay. Now I'm off to find this sex club the family is talking about. I Love you, Captain… I will always love you."

Josephine—eternally succinct. Here it was, I had fought—and I mean fought—an all-out bloody fucking interminable war to protect myself from being judged by everyone in my world. I kept her away because I worried they would treat her like a whore…yeah, "whore."

Her voice message was like an epiphany. She had already assumed their judgment; now it seems so obvious. Why not? She had courted her shadows, she knew all of the parts of herself, and she accepted her own darkness as equally as she had embraced her light.

So why didn't I? Why did I exhaust myself trying to avoid judgment, lose sleep, tear and kick and hate and drink my life away? I wanted to blame it on my family—the Anglo-Saxon Protestants who chose misery above divorce. I made up excuses there would be no acceptance, no religious absolution, no extension of forgiveness, no acts of grace from my circle of family and friends.

I arrogantly thought I had always been protecting Josephine with my lies, the same way I had "protected" Sarah. Josephine does not need protecting. I envision her ripping off the scarlet letter and substituting it with a scarlet gown, shoulders exposed, and slit up the side revealing her thigh taut from four-inch stilettos.

I want to call her and share this image of her dressed in scarlet red so we can laugh at the irony of it all. Then I recall our last phone conversation when I was out of rehab. The exchange was short, her voice distant. Detached. Irritated. Clearly, she was done with the details. Her message was crystal, "Don't come to me with your promises and justifications—I will only accept honesty and courage."

And I let go, again.

And she left, again.

CHAPTER THIRTY-FOUR

It is summertime. My children are chatting with friends on the front lawn. Despite the changes in our family structure, they are content. I do wonder what damage I have done by leaving my marriage. The consequence of my decision has left scars, some temporary, others permanent. I realize, I worked for so many years to provide them with a life of safety and security and then turned their world upside down.

We are conditioned on how to make careers and families, we are not taught how to make a life. Eventually we accept, there can be no other lesson plan than the one we create for ourselves.

While I paint around the window of a newly positioned trim board, I wonder what my children will take away from my example. I worry when they become adults, my daughters will not trust in romantic love. I question if someday they will meet their hearts' desires and offer themselves in barbed wire and security locks.

As parents and spouses, we are constantly negotiating our needs with the needs of those we love. "Personal responsibility" like the kind defined by Ayn Rand is the easy part. I expected my children to have mastered personal responsibility by the age of ten. The difficult part is fulfilling our responsibility to our families, our communities, human kind, and our planet.

Looking through the glass window into my family home, I hear the words of my Italian Grandmother, "Blood is thicker than water; your family comes first, always." I remember bringing our first-born home. Our new baby wrapped in cotton blankets was taken on a tour of the house. In the video I am narrating, "This is the kitchen where Mommy will make you delicious foods to make your belly round and happy."

Then onto the living room, "This is where Daddy will tell you stories and make funny faces."

Climbing the stairs into the bedroom, "Here is where you will dream the loveliest dreams."

My eyes fill with tears and the paint runs from the wood into the window. I climb down from the ladder and wipe my eyes leaving paint smears across my cheeks. In the moment I miss the simplicity of married life, the beauty of my family, together.

There are times I feel completely wrecked by this whole ordeal. Even worse, I feel as though I have wrecked Vince and our children and our beautiful family.

I call Vince at work. When he answers, I am still crying, "I was painting the new trim and I looked through the window into our home and saw the princess birthday parties, game nights, our Christmas tree, and the Saturday morning pancakes, and I felt this wave of sadness."

"Oh, honey," he said "You haven't lost anything. We are still making memories and honoring traditions."

"It's not the same," I sob.

"Jo, sweetheart, in the beginning I worried, too, about the changes that would come. Here's what I know, there will always be changes. And you will always be a part of me. We created a family together, our family will grow and thrive. We will forever be in each other's lives and I will always love you. The children are happy, I am good, and you, love, you are okay. You had the courage to seek out happiness at any cost, to chase a dream, and re-create a life you dared to imagine. We have all learned from you, from your example. In this way our own quests are affirmed, our own dreams validated."

His reassurance makes me cry even harder. "Okay," I say, whispering a quiet, "Thank you," before hanging up.

Vince and I share an extraordinary partnership, one that honors and forgives, persists and lets go.

I climb the stairs to our second story bedroom and let flow tears of regret and tears of gratitude. I lie down on our bed, on my side of what is still our bed. I sacrificed so greatly for a life with Thomas. I forfeited an enduring love for... I do not even know the answer. I lie there in the emptiness of that question, feeling the weight of uncertainty. Throughout my life, decisions have been made. Some decisions were made by others, some were made by obligation or expectation. Other times fear and insecurity made the choice for me. At this point in my life, I only know one thing for certain, my soul is leading the way.

How are we to guess where the future leads? While I am unsure of what waits ahead, I trust in the possibility that comes with risking greatly and surrendering expectations. There is tremendous power in a blank canvas. Who am I to question the path to fulfillment? As the grief passes over me, I rise from my place on our marital bed and splash cold water on my face. After retrieving the paint brush, I climb the ladder to the outside front window of our family home and resume painting.

The children are still on the front lawn where I left them with their friends, giggling and eating popsicles, realities shattered and spirits resilient.

STORE RULES

I remember back to a place long ago in a distant past. It's the usual Tuesday morning and we're having scrambled eggs and waffles at some roadside diner. Josephine studies me for a moment and asks, "What would it mean for you to own this affair?"

"Everyone is not like you, Jo. They don't see love as a moral obligation." I chide with a smirk.

"I don't care about everyone," she replies. "How do you see the decisions we've made?"

I look into those deep dark eyes of hers and tell her the truth, "Our love affair has been the most beautiful disaster of my life."

She brings her hand to pull at the dry skin on her lower lip, a gesture she makes when she gets nervous, still she listens intently for me to continue.

"I tuck my sons into a shared bedroom in their grandparent's basement and drive away wishing they could fall asleep again in the security of my arms. I see it in their eyes…the fear. It's as if everything they knew was a lie and they don't know who or what to trust anymore. The reckless, carefree boy yelp is gone and there is a heaviness none of us can escape."

"Do you feel like you have had to choose between me and the boys?" she asks.

"It's not that I have to choose between you or my sons. I just don't know how to make all four of us the priority. Their lives have been completely uprooted, a new home, a new school. To watch them grieve such losses and to know I am the source. To watch my sons hurt at times feels unbearable…unjustifiable."

I see her swallow and say nothing.

"Remember when you explained relationship karma?"

"Do you mean the store rules: You break it, it belongs to you?"

"Yes," I said. "That's what I feel. This beautiful love we share, it's unlike anything I've ever experienced. The cost though… the betrayals, the losses, all of the damaged relationships with friends and family. I broke them. I can't fix what I have broken, and it belongs to me. Forever. I will forever own this."

She acknowledges my answer and my pain by simply looking directly into my eyes and holding my gaze, softly, tenderly.

The waitress delivers the waffles and eggs. "More coffee, honey?"

"Yes please, thank you."

When the waitress is done pouring the coffee, Josephine rests her hand on my cheek and leans forward to kiss me gently, her tears fall gracefully down my chin.

Josephine knows what many of us have yet to learn. This life we are given is a dream. It's as if we're all caught up in a live drama. Sometimes we are removed enough to watch it all play out. Other times we are the actors on stage.

Josephine isn't a removed critic, she's right there in the audience with us clapping and cheering, enjoying the entertainment. Despite knowing this is simply the next scene in a master design, she surrenders fully to her role on stage.

When the script calls for action, she shows no hesitation. At the appropriate times she delivers her emotion-filled lines expertly, having felt it all.

Once she said to me, "We are either a projection of something past or an expression of something greater and the difference resides simply in our consciousness."

I've thought about this statement for a long time. If I could have seen it as a production, it is possible, I could have played the various parts. Instead I got caught up in the human predicament.

The predicament tells us we are the stars of the show, the screen writer, the production editor and the director. Instead I tried to control the outcomes, tried to mitigate the damage, and attached myself to roles I could no longer fulfill. The homemade armor and cardboard sword was not mine to wear, neither was the pirate hat. Not now. Not anymore.

CHAPTER THIRTY-FIVE

Years ago, my husband was climbing into bed after I had just fallen asleep. In that brief space where the subconscious asserts control over the conscious filter I called out, "Who are you and what gifts do you bring?" He laughed so hard I awoke with a startle. He repeated what I had just said and, still chuckling, teased, "Now that just sums it up."

I have curiously entered the online dating world. It appeals to my sense of efficiency as my time is limited and my interest insufficient. For the first time since I was fifteen, I am completely available. I see every man as a new world, a new context to me, and I get to witness myself in these unfamiliar places.

Internet dating also aligns with my love of games. When eBay first hit the market, early in my development, I nearly had to see a therapist. I was addicted to a sense of "winning" regardless of how much I had to spend on the "winning" bid.

Eventually the credit card bills started rolling in and I quickly realized this "game" was too expensive. Yet with the same gaming spirit, I have headed off into the world of Match.com and E-Harmony.

Fred 1: Drinks—Nice guy. Made me laugh. Great conversation. Good heart with a wild streak. He would be a perfect match if he were taller and his nose smaller. The kissing was full-on, bold. He invites me back up to his place. (His first mistake of the evening.)

Fred 2: Sushi—Engineer. Has the right politics. Loving father. Recently divorced and still wounded. He drinks too much and gets too inebriated to make the one hour drive home. I am still considering right up until the kiss, little baby pecks. I hate him for those kisses. I set him up on the sofa. He talks his way into my bed. I spend the remainder of the evening removing his hand from my ass. In the morning I give him a baby peck goodbye and never talk to him again.

Fred 3: Drinks—Total pimp. He scolds me for not giving him a second date.

Fred 4: Coffee—Loaded. Older than he declares on his profile and never married. I can tell it will not work, ever. Still there is something familiar and comforting about him. The second date is dinner. We talk for three hours. I learn everything there is to know about him.

Fred 5: Bar meet-up—One hot daddy! I had plans but he refused to wait the two weeks until I had an opening in my schedule. I agree to let him meet up with me during karaoke night with friends. When he arrives, I am two drinks into the warm fluid center. We spend all night discussing why our relationship will never work, naked, and taking turns riding each other.

Fred 6: Brunch—Bingo! He is a brilliant business owner, world traveler, fly-fisherman, witty, kind, and a traditionalist. He is 13 years older. I know him by the stories he tells of his childhood: "the fixer," "the caretaker," "the leader." I love him instantly. He lusts me. We go on walks, take bike rides, and go patio dining. He has shoulders like my great-uncle's and hands like a brick layer. The same shoulders and hands that built homes, shielded children from danger, and cultivated the fields and the folds of their wives. He wants to build me a home and take me traveling. I want that, too. He wants to come home to me each night curled in his bed and wake each morning with his name branded on my fair skin. Only, I am the kind of woman a man waits up for. He cannot forego his claim or cede his territory, nor can I. We square off, two courageous warriors, battle-worn and fatigued, each consenting to isolation before compromise.

Fred 7: I can't remember—Still pining over Fred 6.

Fred 8: Steak Dinner—Pictures are deceiving. More money than he knows what to do with. More arrogance than I know what to do with. Is asshole a prerequisite to being rich? Tolstoy was right in this case. Wealth corrupts, especially the soul.

Fred 9: Lunch—Followed by a spontaneous weekend gambling. I learn how to play Blackjack and win $300. Next month I see him again, in the newspaper pictured in an orange jumpsuit. The article explains it is a preliminary hearing where he is charged with successfully contracting the brutal murder of his ex-wife.

My Internet dating game is over.

LOVE AND LOSS

Josephine.

Those eyes....

God, how her gypsy soul and radiant defiance consumes me still—unattainable, not just to me, to anyone. She is far too free, too wild for reins. She's the modern day Don Juanita with no desire for conquests of her own. Her only wish is to escape the bonds, even the bonds of love, if they limit her creativity or imagination. Josephine will not be conquered.

The men, all of them...so effortlessly drawn to a vitality they can't understand. They falter in her presence. I've seen it again and again. They try to take it all in—the raw strength and bold femininity. It's too much. I watch them—the sudden look in their eyes when they realize they have been missing something. They roll back ever so slightly on their heels, not quite understanding what just happened.

I've seen them reach for some sort of center, a moment of steadiness to get a grasp on their inexplicable desire and yearning. They search themselves, knowing they can't define it—realizing in the deepest part of themselves whatever they need, flows from Josephine like water from a mountain spring.

The beauty of Mark Antony and Cleopatra is how death interceded before the realities of love could be fully played out. Yet, in love, there really never is an ending. It is fluid like a mighty river ebbing and flowing, occasionally stalling in small eddies, only to break free again. Eventually, the water meets with the vast ocean and mixes with new life, waiting its turn to evaporate into the oneness. Or so you think until a cumulus cloud, fully sodden, abandons her raindrops meeting with the river once again. There is no point of origin, or any end. It is a never ending continuum traversing air and sea.

There are no fairy tales and love is eternal.

CHAPTER THIRTY-SIX

I am in Portland, presenting at a conference beginning tomorrow. The scene change is welcome. It has been a rough fall.

Thomas had two years of sobriety when he relapsed again. The last time I saw him I had driven to his apartment after a phone call. I could hear the slur in his words and knew before I even arrived he had relapsed. I kept him on the phone the entire drive there, my heart exploding in my chest. It took him a couple of minutes to answer the door. He finally answered still holding the phone in his hands with this grin like he was both surprised and happy to see me. No words were spoken as I walked past him standing there barefoot and shirtless in a pair of jeans I knew he had just scrambled into.

The half-pint plastic bottle of vodka was stashed in a gym duffle by the bedroom door. It was the cheap kind and it was completely empty. Thomas had settled himself on his bed and watched as I rifled through his things looking for what we both knew was waiting there hidden. The only words I spoke throughout the entire event was when I handed him his phone and told him to call his sponsor. My body was perched on the edge as I listened to the conversation. Tears fell silently defeated. When I was sufficiently convinced his sponsor had been apprised of the situation, I rose from the bed, kissed Thomas on the forehead and left the apartment.

I called my father on the return drive home. "Dad," I asked, my voice pleading, "I love him so much and I know he loves me, what if I could accept him with this disease?"

"It only gets worse, Josephine."

I knew he was right. I knew that to stay in this relationship would again lock me into a role of caregiver, problem-solver, and mess manager. I hadn't left my marriage because I was in love. I hadn't said goodbye to my husband because it was a wise choice. I made the leap of faith into Thomas' arms because of something primitive within me. A long held secret wish there would be someone in the world to nurture me, to protect me from the dangers that come with being alive. I so badly wanted a man who would help me to feel safe in this world. A man who did not make messes; who could solve his own problems. Most importantly, I wanted a partner who could navigate the very difficult balance between autonomy and intimacy.

I knew, as I knew from the beginning, I can never have peace where alcoholism and addiction are present. My brain decided it was time to go and my heart broke, again. I tucked my secret wish into the hidden recesses where it resides still. My foot pressed harder against the gas pedal as I directed my gaze forward, beyond the tears, focused only on the two beams lighting the way against the uncertain darkness.

Vince settled into a new relationship, the first one since our separation more than three years ago. He waited several months before telling me. I knew and felt his absence and of course was drawn back toward him. That door is closed.

The enlightened part of me is grateful that he has found love again. The ego part of me wants to scratch her eyes out. I do the only thing I can and cry my way to acceptance.

This lovely fall morning I ride the Max, Portland's light rail. It is crowded with people and speeds forward and then lurches to a stop noisily. I had lunch in the plaza where a homeless protégé played the violin barefoot. Portland has street corners stacked with food carts. Antarctica is the only continent not represented. The food carts resemble shantytowns. On a single square block I counted twenty-four carts, including Thai, Greek, Mexican, Indian, Asian, and Ital-

ian. I ordered Cuban and wiped spicy pulled pork juices as they ran down my chin.

As I used the plastic utensils to spoon cilantro rice and black beans into my mouth, I scanned the crowd, hoping no one was watching my spectacle of gluttony. When I reached the white Styrofoam bottom, only the fried plantains were left staring back at me. I shrugged my shoulders, listened intently to the cry of the violin, and ate those, too. If I lived here, I would try a new food cart each day until I had them all, and then I would start all over!

The Max runs through a tunnel and includes a stop at the Japanese Garden. As I climb the stairs a trolley is magically waiting to take me to the garden's entrance. From the first steps inside, I understand this is a spiritual place. Even the visitors are transformed.

Descriptions are completely inadequate here. Everything is lush green or dark earth. The trees and plants are all shapes and textures, shades and hues. There are paths and archways, benches and sculptures. Streams and ponds meander together and water features emerge and disappear filling the air with sounds of rhythmic tapping.

I find I am particularly attracted to the bubbling brooks and cascading waterfalls. These are new smells of earth in its optimal state, all of the elements singing together in harmonious rapture. I am listening to the water splash from a waterfall into a dark pool when a black woman with a colorful head scarf sits next to me. She is a full-bodied, round woman and dark as the night with lighter freckles appearing like lightning bugs across her nose and cheeks. I smile and she pats me reassuringly on the knee as if we have been friends throughout multiple lifetimes. The two of us sit in silence for some time, listening to the birds' chatter. Her strength is witnessed in her straight posture; her wisdom evident in the way her eyes attend to the details of our setting.

I wonder aloud, "What is it that draws us to water?" without expecting a reply.

"It is moving and breathing and changing. It is completely alive," she answers simply.

I recognize the experience I have been exploring all along...the ex-

perience of a life fully expressed. Like the water, I long to break free of the stagnation, to breathe oxygen into the dead parts, and to venture on untraveled paths over earth and soul.

With both of our eyes cast in the direction of the falling water she proceeds, "Instead of teaching our children they will fall in love and it will last forever, we can teach them they will have many loves, some permanent, some not. We can show them how we learn the most about ourselves in loving and accepting loss."

When she stands to leave I question if this is an Isabelle Allende moment; have I conjured this woman from my imagination?

I can see her so vividly though, the bright white of her eyes, her supple roundness. Her bracelets jingle as she turns northward and her sweet scent of jasmine lingers with me. While she is still within earshot I reply, "Thank you."

She turns back towards me and blesses me with a smile.

We learn things, important things, when we leave our comfortable lives. We grow and stretch in ways we did not know were possible. If you do not learn your truth, you cannot tell the truth.

Throughout this journey I am learning. I can construct ornamental gates to the miracles in the outside world, I can seep my own hallowed spaces into the ordinary.

I know which parts to protect, and I also know the ever abundant source from which love flows eternal. I am remembering not to trample the consecrated spaces of others and how to clear out the overgrowth and make way for sunlight.

Eventually I too rise from the spot in front of the water falls and travel further down the path until I reach a fire sculpture. The flames are small and dance wildly in colors between orange, gold, and blue.

I think back on these last seven years. Each loss becomes another log on the fire. I watch the flames burn all of my attachments away to nothing. I let go of the golden carriage and Cinderella promises. I fuel the blaze with rocking chairs I once occupied and beds where I had slept. I toss in the beauty and tragedy of yesterday because re-

gardless, it is in the past.

I watch the flames leap higher and forfeit the insecurities of childhood, along with any fears for tomorrow. I study the embers' glow and whisper a quiet prayer for my children on their own path to freedom. I step closer to the flames, removing my remaining security blankets and let the fire consume those, too.

For the first time in my life, I stand bare and alone, unafraid, with the reflection of the flames dancing on eyes wide open, corners of mouth turned skyward.

I thought this was going to be another love story. Instead it is the story of liberation...my own. Freedom is the decision to look at the moment and see the beauty and the suffering and accept them both equally with outstretched arms. It requires an atonement with the darkest parts of ourselves and a willingness to stand naked in the light places in full acceptance of both.

Perhaps I could have gotten here another way. Some people travel long distances on pilgrimages to holy places. I learned the holy places reside within, and the treasures to be revealed are there, too, right along with the heartbreak and the splendor.

I have awakened to my own life and it looks like breathing it all in, and letting it all go, every fleeting moment.

As the sun descends over the Japanese Garden and the hour of required departure draws near, I bid farewell to the meandering stream, whose only course is to travel forward, I turn away from the dancing flames, the memory of old attachments, feeling the red hot of my own heart beating, and the quiet knowing we are all, each one of us, destined for ashes anyway.

THE END

It's morning again, early. I never used to wake before dawn. Not for anything, even while the kids were bustling about bickering and losing their shoes while my ex-wife slammed cupboards in frustration because they were running so late. Maybe that is the reason why I slept.

Each day now, it's the silence that wakes me, the stillness; the absence of everything. When it arrives on the midst of a twilight dream of Josephine, as it often does, I instinctively reach for her...her empty place awakens me. I cannot think of where she is. Then the waves recede...I remember she is gone. And I lay in the darkness and breathe in the silence.

It is unfathomable to me. Not even that she left, or why. It is unfathomable to me how when she said goodbye, I simply let Josephine pull her hand free from mine.

All the moments we had shared, the soaring adventures, the tenderness, the passion and purity of love...gone...without any fight or argument at all.

What was left in the end was acceptance—a willingness to trust and let go.

Maybe this was an act of love in itself. From each of us.

Not that it would have mattered. Nothing I could have said would have changed anything. There is a place where words have no meaning anymore.

I had already lost Josephine, it began with losing me.

I think back to the last time we made love together. It was

not frenetic and heat passionate, but tender, soft, and pure. She undressed and gently guided me towards her. We stared into each other's eyes, entranced in a deep slow rhythm.

I whispered, "My love," and she smiled, never losing her gaze. I watched her eyes as her breath caught and she released and then she watched mine. I held my hand to her heart, ran my cheek against the softness of her belly, and wished for a different ending.

Made in the
USA
Columbia, SC

79612562R00111